SAP Business Explorer (BEx) Tools

Peter Scott

W9-BAM-422

Contents

Acknowledgements

This book is dedicated to my parents, Don and Valorie, who have always been there to support and motivate me at every turn and to my lovely wife, Bobbi, who inspires me each and every day of my life. I love you.

1 Fundamentals of BW Reporting

1.1 Basics of Data Warehousing

For many reasons, information was once nearly impossible to extract from applications. Corporate systems were unconnected, little historical information could be stored, and the data that was stored was often inaccessible. These difficulties led to the concept of a *Data Warehouse* (DW).

Put simply, a data warehouse serves as a decision support environment where corporate data can be quickly summarized at different operational levels.

Data warehousing is the process of choosing, migrating, cleaning, transforming, and storing data from disparate systems into one common location, whereby users can easily extract and analyze information for management decisions.

A data warehouse is also commonly referred to as a:

- Data Mart
- Corporate Information Factory (CIF)
- Decision Support System (DSS)
- Business Intelligence (BI)
- Business Warehouse (BW)

One of the largest sources of data is typically an Enterprise Resource Planning (ERP) system. The process of migrating data from an ERP system to a data warehouse is usually referred to as *Extraction, Transformation, and Loading* (ETL).

The multidimensional analysis offered by a data warehouse, which enables DW users to analyze data trends, exceptions, and variances of interest is called *Online Analytical Processing* (OLAP). Typical OLAP is used to answer questions such as:

- What was my best selling product in January?
- What was the total company revenue for 2005?
- Why was I over my budget in March?
- What are my year-to-date sales figures?
- How will my year-end look?

1.2 Basics of BW Design

SAP Business Information Warehouse (SAP BW) is an end-to-end data warehousing solution that is usually built on a three-tier environment that consists of a Development (DEV), Test (Quality Assurance, QA), and Production (PROD) server. This three-tier configuration separates development work from a live system, and allows for sufficient testing with real data in the QA system. Enhancements are transported through a well-defined process that moves from DEV to QA for testing, and then from DEV to PROD, where BW users can access them.

SAP BW has a three-tiered architecture, which consists of the following layers. Figure 1.1 summarizes the architecture. The layers of the architecture are seen below:

- **Presentation layer**
  Consists of the SAP Business Explorer (BEx) tools such as BEx Analyzer and BEx Browser.
- **Database layer**
  Consists of InfoCubes, Operational Data Stores (ODS), MultiCubes, and Master Data Objects that can be reported on. This layer also includes the Administrator Workbench.
- **Source Systems layer**
  Consists of ERP systems, legacy systems, text files, or another SAP BW environment.

All SAP BW queries are constructed via using BEx tools, which request data from the BW database. The BW database follows an ETL process to populate InfoCubes, ODS, MultiCubes, and Master Data.

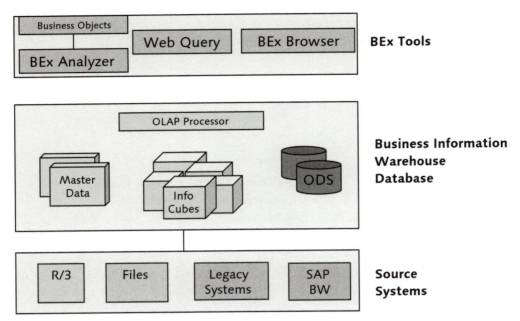

Figure 1.1   High-Level BW Architecture

Objects for which queries can be created against or executed on using BEx tools are collectively referred to as *InfoProviders*. An *InfoCube*, which is a type of InfoProvider, is a subset or collection of data from the BW database that has relationships, which allow users to report on many things simultaneously.

You define queries with the *BEx Query Designer*. You can display them as a BW web report using a web browser, or view them within a Microsoft Excel Workbook with the BEx Analyzer.

Many queries can be built from a single InfoProvider. A single query definition has a one-to-one relationship with its InfoProvider. The query results from a query definition are displayed on a web page, or in the BEx Analyzer. You can format and store query results with many different views, which can result in a many-to-one relationship between a query definition and the formatted query results. Figure 1.2 displays these relationships.

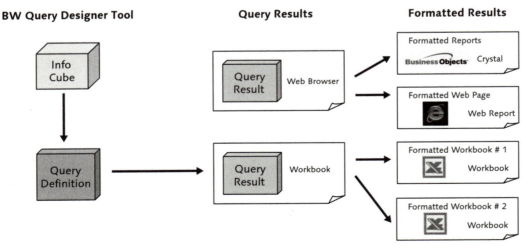

Figure 1.2   Relationship Among InfoProvider, Query Definition, and Formatted Query Results

1.3 Business Explorer (BEx) Tools

SAP BEx reporting tools allow users to create, locate, execute, view, format, manage, schedule and precalculate reports. The primary BEx tools include:

▶ BEx Browser
▶ BEx Analyzer
▶ BEx Query Designer
▶ BEx Web Application Designer
▶ Reporting Agent
▶ Download Scheduler

All the BEx tools in SAP BW are installed on a client workstation using the SAP GUI installation disc.

The *BEx Browser* is a graphical desktop-like tool, from where you can launch queries and workbooks and categorize them into **Roles**, **Favorites**, and **Folders**. The BEx Browser also incorporates standard shortcut functionality, which enables you to access documents, Windows applications, Internet URLs, and SAP R/3 transactions from a single interface. The BEx Browser allows users to create folders to organize their content. Figure 1.3 illustrates how BW content can be linked with other business tools in the BEx Browser.

The BEx Browser toolbar (shown in Figure 1.4) contains the following icons:

▶ Exit
▶ Save
▶ Refresh
▶ Start Business Explorer Analyzer
▶ Find
▶ New Folder
▶ Delete
▶ About SAP BW Browser
▶ Help

Figure 1.4 BEx Browser Toolbar

You create content within the BEx Browser on the right side of the screen. Right-clicking on a blank part of the screen displays a context menu with several options. You

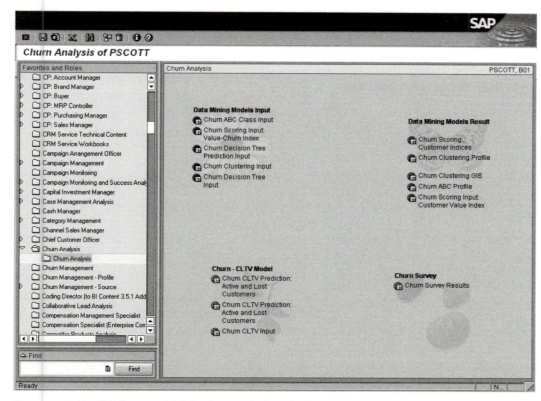

Figure 1.3 Linking BW Content with Other Business Tools in the BEx Browser

can create the following links within a folder (Figure 1.5 displays the available options):

- ▶ Folder
- ▶ Workbook
- ▶ Internet Address (URL)
- ▶ SAP Transaction
- ▶ Document (Word, PowerPoint)
- ▶ Shortcut (to other applications on a local PC)

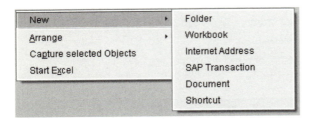

Figure 1.5 Adding New Content to a Folder

Each folder created for a **role** or **user Favorites** can be further customized by assigning a background symbol and color, which appear to be translucent. There are eight backgrounds and colors, each of which has a nature theme, from which to choose.

To customize folder options, right-click on a folder on the right side of the BEx Browser window and select **Choose symbol and color**. The graphical options are displayed in Figure 1.6.

Figure 1.6 Folders Customized with Background Symbol and Color

The *BEx Analyzer* is the primary reporting environment for SAP BW. Most users find it very intuitive because it is integrated with Microsoft Excel. You can add Excel calculations, notes, charts and graphics to a single worksheet and insert multiple reports into a workbook, thereby cre-

ating a package of reports. The BEx Analyzer combines the power of OLAP with all the Excel functionality. You can also use *Visual Basic for Applications* (VBA).

The *BEx Query Designer* is a standalone application that enables users to build complex query definitions without using programming. All subsequent BW reporting and analysis is based on query definitions. The BEx Query Designer is displayed in Figure 1.7.

The BEx Query Designer can be launched from the **Start** menu of a Windows PC, or from the BEx Analyzer, the BEx Web Application Designer, or Crystal Reports.

The *BEx Web Application Designer* (WAD) is a desktop application that is very similar to other web page authoring tools. For example, BEx WAD and Microsoft FrontPage, as well as Dreamweaver, are alike in that they all enable you to use a WYSIWYG environment when launching a website. One unique feature of the WAD is that it enables you to incorporate BW data and predefined BW objects, along with standard HTML code and web design application programming interfaces (APIs).

The *Reporting Agent* allows you to schedule various reporting functions in the background during non-peak times. Furthermore, you can precalculate all web templates created with the WAD. The advantage here is that it shortens the wait time for users and reduces the workload on the servers. You'll find the Reporting Agent within the Administrator Workbench. You can access it directly using the **RSREP** Transaction. The Reporting Agent's most commonly used functions are:

- ▶ Execute and Analyze Exception Reports
- ▶ Print Reports
- ▶ Precalculate Web Templates

The Reporting Agent is divided into three panes:

- ▶ Functions pane
- ▶ Settings pane
- ▶ Scheduling pane

You use the same process for all functions. The **Settings** pane is used to navigate through a folder structure to find a query definition. Once located, you must enter specific settings that pertain to the highlighted function (e.g., Printing). To establish new settings for a query, right-click on the name of the query and choose **New Setting** (see Figure 1.8).

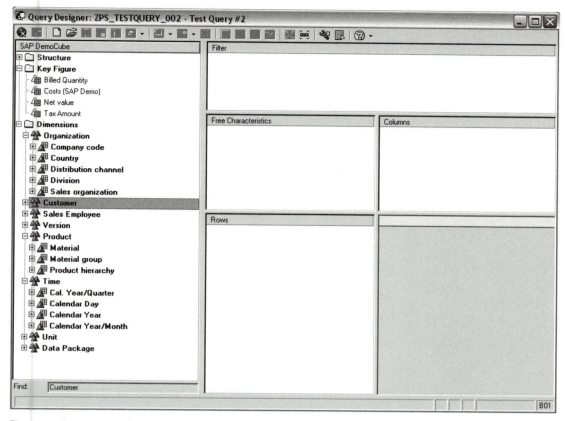

Figure 1.7 Creating Complex Queries Without Programming

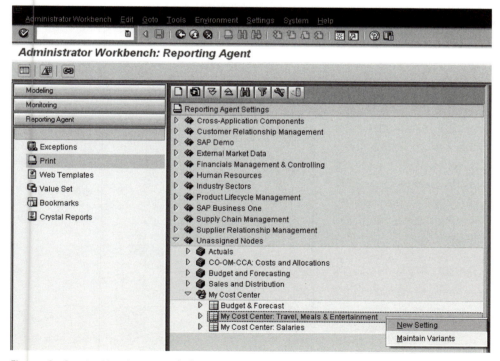

Figure 1.8 Creating New Settings with the Reporting Agent

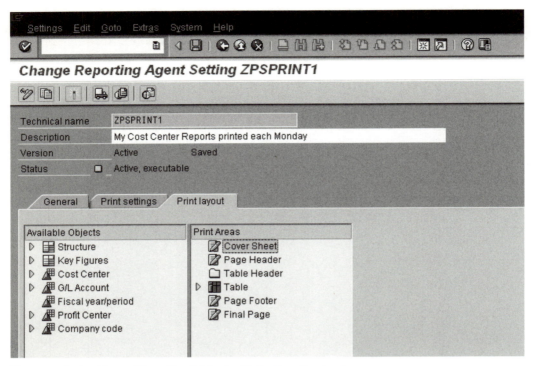

Figure 1.9 Customizing and Formatting Printouts with the Reporting Agent

Each new setting requires a **Technical name** and a **Description**. Settings also allow for some layout and distribution options. Depending on the function selected, these options vary. For example, the **Print** function allows a user to build a cover sheet, page header, and page footer, and design a layout template for the printed data. The printing options are shown in Figure 1.9.

Once the settings are specified, they must be saved and activated. The keyboard shortcut to save changes is **Ctrl+S** and the shortcut to activate changes is **Ctrl+F3**. A green status light will confirm that a Reporting Agent setting has been saved and is now executable.

The **Scheduling** pane is used to generate a scheduling package that will contain the details of the query setting created earlier. A technical name and description are required for each new scheduling package.

You attach a Reporting Agent setting for a particular query to a scheduling package by dragging and dropping the setting from the **Settings** pane to the package in the **Scheduling** pane.

To schedule a package, right-click on the name of the package and select **Schedule** (see Figure 1.10).

Choosing a start condition that will trigger the package to be executed completes the scheduling process. You can schedule a package to run:

- Immediately
- At a specific date and time
- On a periodic schedule (Daily, Monthly, Weekly)
- After a particular system event
- After a particular job

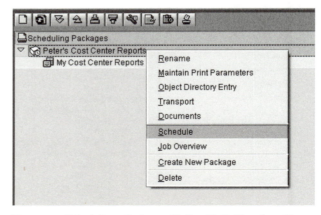

Figure 1.10 Scheduling a Package with Specific Settings for a Query Definition

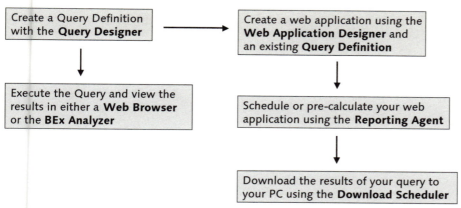

Figure 1.11 BEx Tools Workflow

Once the start condition is specified, the package is saved. Scheduled packages can be monitored from the **Job Overview** screen.

Because the Reporting Agent is part of the *Administrator Workbench*, you should ensure that it is not deployed to all BW users. A strategy that limits development work in the Reporting Agent to a handful of power users is preferable. Furthermore, you must ensure that the packages created with the Reporting Agent are monitored periodically for performance reasons, especially since an incorrectly defined package can run for a long time and therefore monopolize valuable system resources. You should also make certain that scheduling packages are inserted into process chains. To do this, use the Process Chain Maintenance transaction code **RSPC**.

The *BEx Download Scheduler* is a desktop application that downloads, or schedules a time for the download, precalculated HTML pages, or Excel workbooks to a local PC. These pages are precalculated using the Reporting Agent. The BEx Download Scheduler tool is typically accessed from the Windows **Start** menu under **Programs · Business Explorer · Download Scheduler**.

The Download Scheduler wizard helps users to find packages assigned to their user ID, and places the results of these packages into designated folders on the users' PCs. The output of the report can also be formatted for a PDA device.

The overall workflow for using all the various BEx tools is shown in Figure 1.11. The most basic reporting is accomplished by using the BEx Query Designer and the BEx Analyzer. An alternative or complimentary reporting strategy to just using the BEx Analyzer is to use web-based reporting. With web reporting, you don't have to install any software on a user's PC, which is why this alternative is known as a "zero-footprint" solution. Query designers can publish formatted, graphical reports using the *BEx Web Application Designer* and distribute these reports via URLs or a pre-existing intranet portal. High-end formatting can be achieved by leveraging the Reporting Agent, Download Scheduler, or via integration with Crystal Reports.

1.4 Summary

SAP BW has evolved into a full-fledged Data Warehouse. The BEx tools allow users with diverse backgrounds to effectively access data in a timely manner. Queries are defined using the BEx Query Designer and analyzed within the BEx Analyzer or BEx Web Applications. Additional formatting can be achieved with the BEx Web Application Designer or via BW's integration with Crystal Reports. The next chapter will look at the BEx Query Designer in detail.

2 The BEx Query Designer

2.1 Overview of the BEx Query Designer

The Business Explorer (BEx) Query Designer is a stand-alone application accessed from the Business Explorer within a Windows **Start** menu. To access the BEx Query Designer, use the menu path **Start · All Programs · Business Explorer · Query Designer** (see Figure 2.1).

> **Note:** The specific menu path may differ, depending on the installation version of the SAP GUI software.

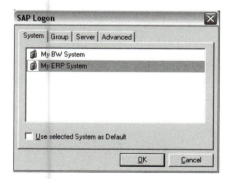

Figure 2.1 Navigating to the BEx Query Designer

Launching the Query Designer prompts you to log on to a specific SAP BW system (see Figure 2.2).

Figure 2.2 Selecting a BW Environment from the SAP Logon Pad

From the **SAP Logon** pad, in the **System** tab, select the appropriate BW environment, and click **OK**.

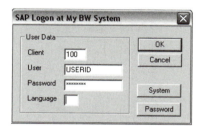

Figure 2.3 Logging On to SAP BW

The BW system then prompts you for valid logon credentials (see Figure 2.3). Enter the following information:

- ▶ **Client** (#)
- ▶ **User** (ID)
- ▶ **Password**
- ▶ **Language** (2-digit code. "EN" — English, "FR" — French)

The initial view of the BEx Query Designer is displayed in Figure 2.4.

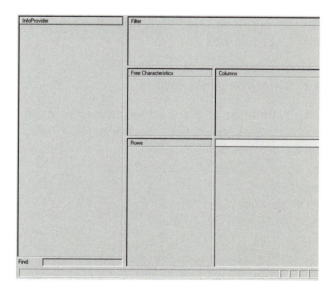

Figure 2.4 Initial View of BEx Query Designer

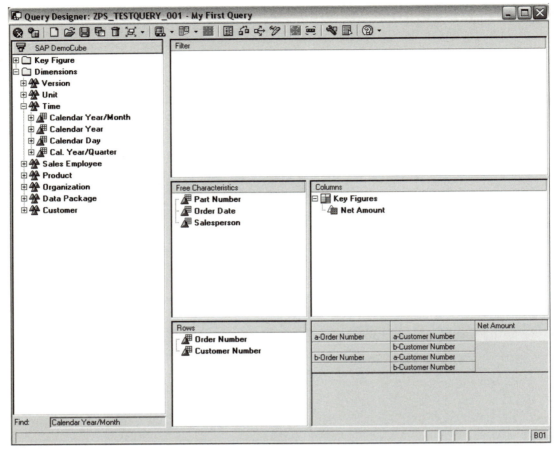

Figure 2.5   BEx Query Designer Panes

Once you have entered the required information, click **OK**. The BEx Query Designer is displayed in a new window (see Figure 2.5).

2.2   Query Designer Layout

The Query Designer is a graphical standalone application that allows datasets to be accessed via InfoProviders. Examples of InfoProviders are:

▶ Operational Data Stores (ODS objects)
▶ InfoCubes
▶ Master Data
▶ MultiProviders (MultiCubes)

Query definitions are created from InfoProviders. No programming knowledge is required to create a query. Users can simply drag and drop specific elements from

an InfoProvider and build an entire query definition using the BEx Query Designer toolbar.

In addition to the toolbar, six panes make up the BEx Query Designer. The left-most pane of the Query Designer, which displays all data available for a particular InfoProvider, is considered to be the *source* pane. The five remaining panes are *destination* panes, which are used to create and format a query definition. The following panes constitute these destination panes:

▶ **Filter**
▶ **Free Characteristics**
▶ **Columns**
▶ **Rows**
▶ **Preview** (not labeled)

Selecting and combining InfoObjects from an InfoProvider and placing them in specific destination panes determines the default layout of a report. InfoObjects can be either characteristics or key figures.

Table 2.1 lists these BEx Query Designer panes and describes each of their respective behaviors.

BEx Query Designer Panes	Behavior
InfoProvider Pane	Provides a hierarchical listing of all structures, characteristics, variables, and key figures available from a particular InfoProvider (InfoCube, ODS, Multi-Cube). These elements are the building blocks for a new query definition.
Filter Pane	Characteristics placed in the Filter pane are never displayed in the output of a report. In general, InfoObjects placed in this pane are restricted by specific values; for example, placing Calendar Year in the Filter pane and restricting the InfoObject to 2006.
Free Characteristics Pane	InfoObjects placed in the Free Characteristics pane are added to a report, but are not displayed in the report output unless this is requested by a user. This allows a query definition to be constructed with numerous fields that can be displayed, but only when requested by the user.
Columns Pane	InfoObjects placed in the Columns pane are added to a report and displayed by default. Characteristics and key figures can be combined in this pane.
Rows Pane	InfoObjects placed in the Rows pane are added to a report and displayed by default. Characteristics and key figures can be combined in this pane.
Preview Pane	The Preview pane provides a very basic representation of a report template. Only objects found in the Rows and Columns panes will appear in the Preview pane.

Table 2.1 Summary of BEx Query Designer Panes

In summary, placing objects from an InfoProvider into the various destination panes builds a default view of a report (anything in the Rows and Columns), and allows for additional information to be presented if it is wanted (**Free Characteristics**). Users can navigate to a query definition to build their own version of a report by deciding what objects they would like to see and in what particular order they want these objects to appear. They can achieve this specified order by shuffling InfoObjects found in the **Rows**, **Columns**, and **Free Characteristics**

panes. Any characteristics placed in the Filter pane are not available for users to display in their report output.

A query definition is constructed with the following objects in each pane:

▶ **Free Characteristics** Pane
  ▶ Part Number (Characteristic)
  ▶ Order Date (Characteristic)
  ▶ Salesperson (Characteristic)
▶ **Rows** Pane
  ▶ Order Number (Characteristic)
  ▶ Customer Number (Characteristic)
▶ **Columns** Pane
  ▶ Net Amount (Key Figures)

The query definition for this example is displayed within the BEx Query Designer tool (see Figure 2.6).

Figure 2.6 BEx Query Designer Toolbar

The flexibility of a query definition is determined by the contents of the **Free Characteristics pane**. By default, the report will display only the Order Number, Customer Number, and Net Amount. The Order Date is not available in the initial report result; however, a user can display it easily with just the click of a mouse. Another user may require that the salesperson be listed in the report output. Consequently, many users can employ the same basic report, by simply leveraging additional information that was placed in the **Free Characteristics** pane.

2.3 Using the BEx Query Designer Toolbar

The BEx Query Designer toolbar consists of the following icons:

▶ Exit Query
▶ Display Query on the Web
▶ New Query
▶ Open Query
▶ Save Query
▶ Save Query As
▶ Delete Query
▶ Publish
▶ Exception
▶ Condition

- ▶ Define Cells
- ▶ Query Properties
- ▶ Check Query
- ▶ Query Where-Used List
- ▶ Display/Change Mode
- ▶ Change Query (Global Definition)
- ▶ Table Display
- ▶ Technical Names
- ▶ Context Menu
- ▶ Help

Each of these icons will be discussed throughout this chapter. Depending on the current state of a query definition, certain icons and functionality may not be available. When a specific icon or tool is not available, the icon will be grayed-out. As was shown in Figure 2.6, the **Change Query (Global Definition)** icon and the **Table Display** icon are not accessible.

2.4 Accessing InfoProviders

Launching the BEx Query Designer and logging on to the preferred SAP BW environment is the first step in creating a query definition. The next step requires a user to pick a certain functional area of the BW database, usually designated by an InfoCube, which contains information of interest (see Figure 2.7).

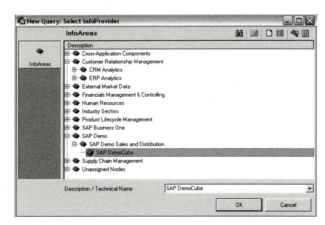

Figure 2.7 Finding Available InfoProviders in InfoAreas

InfoCubes are the preferred InfoProvider to report on. They offer better performance than Operational Data Stores (ODS), and contain multiple dimensions that

make them more useful to business analysts for building reports.

To access an InfoProvider, click on the **New Query** icon in the BEx Query Designer toolbar. A pop-up window opens and displays all available InfoProviders to a user. Depending on standard SAP roles and security profiles, each user may see only a subset of all the available InfoCubes, ODS objects, and MultiCubes. InfoProviders are grouped by InfoAreas, which are simply folders that allow InfoProviders with similar functional data to be grouped together.

Navigate through the folder structure until you locate the InfoProvider that you want. Double-clicking on an individual InfoCube or ODS will bring it into the Query Designer.

> **Note:** If the description or technical name of a particular InfoProvider is well known, you can use this text as a search string to navigate through the InfoArea hierarchy quickly. To search for a specific cube, click on the **Find** icon (pair of binoculars) located in the toolbar of the **Select InfoProvider** window (see Figure 2.8).

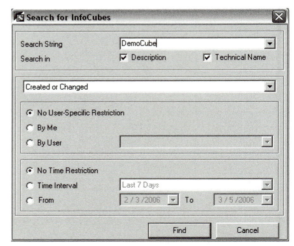

Figure 2.8 Search for InfoCubes

An InfoProvider loaded into the Query Designer appears in the left-most pane of the screen (see Figure 2.9). It is structured into the three most high-level folders:

- ▶ Key Figures
- ▶ Dimensions
- ▶ Structures

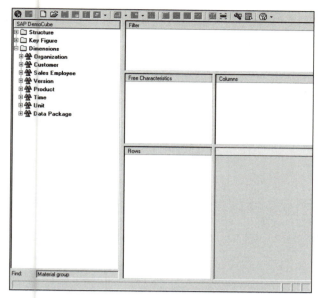

Figure 2.9 Open InfoProvider Displayed in Left Pane of Query Designer

Examples of *Key Figures* are quantities, amounts, and values. *Dimensions* are logical groupings of characteristics that fit together well. A dimension labeled as "Customer" will typically include things like Customer Number, Sold-to Party, and Country. *Characteristics* are qualitative fields that describe the key figures. Cost Center and Sales Region are other examples of characteristics.

Structures are created by query designers after an InfoProvider has been made available. Because structures are reusable, they allow work that has been completed in one query to be used by other queries. A combination of characteristics and key figures, in a particular order, with specific filters can be saved back to the InfoProvider as a structure.

When future queries are developed from the InfoProvider, you can add the reusable structure to a new query with a simple drag and drop. This allows for the rapid development of queries that use common sets of columns or rows. It also facilitates the easy maintenance of multiple queries; for instance, adjusting the structure members for a single query will immediately update all queries that use the same row or column structure.

Updating all the queries using a common structure is not always wanted or recommended. Often it can be helpful to use an existing structure to expedite query development and then to sever all ties to this global

structure. Removing the reference will protect a query from unwanted future changes when the structure is changed. To remove a reference, right-click on a structure in a query definition (see Figure 2.10) and select **Remove Reference**.

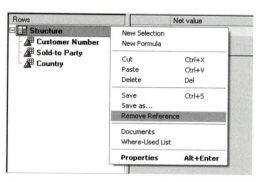

Figure 2.10 Removing a Global Reference to a Reusable Structure

To add a structure, key figure, or characteristic to a query definition, simply drag and drop the item from the InfoProvider source pane to the appropriate destination pane. To remove an item from a query definition, highlight the selected item and press **Delete** or drag and drop the item back to the InfoProvider source pane. Figure 2.11 on page 16 shows the beginnings of a Query Definition.

2.5 Creating a Basic Query Definition

The following steps outline a methodology for developing a query and take into account the underlying functionality and efficiency considerations of the BEx Query Designer.

1. Click on the **New Query** icon in the BEx Query Designer toolbar.
2. Select the InfoProvider that you want.
3. Drag and drop pre-existing structures to the **Rows** pane or **Columns** pane.
4. Drag and drop characteristics to the **Rows**, **Filter**, or **Free Characteristics** panes.
5. Restrict characteristics.
6. Format each characteristic found in the **Rows**, **Filter**, or **Free Characteristics** panes.
7. Drag and drop key figures to the **Columns** pane.
8. Create any required restricted key figures.
9. Create any required calculated key figures.
10. Format each key figure in the **Columns** pane.

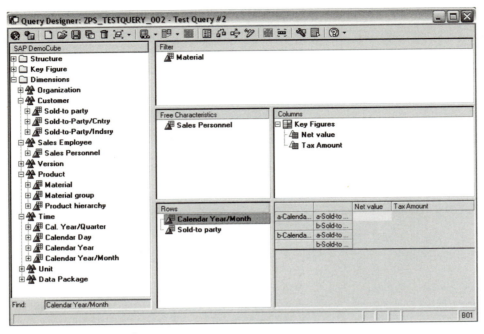

Figure 2.11   Basic Query Definition

11. Add characteristic value variables for characteristics found in the **Rows**, **Filter**, or **Free Characteristics** panes.

12. Click on the **Exception** icon in the BEx Query Designer toolbar to define exceptions.

13. Click on the **Condition** icon in the BEx Query Designer toolbar to define conditions.

14. Click on the **Query Properties** icon in the BEx Query Designer toolbar to adjust query properties.

15. Click on the **Check Query** icon in the BEx Query Designer toolbar to check the query syntax.

16. Save the query with the **Save Query** icon in the BEx Query Designer toolbar.

17. Click on the **Display Query on the Web** icon in the BEx Query Designer toolbar to execute and test the query.

18. Click on the **Publish** icon in the BEx Query Designer toolbar to publish the query.

SAP BW categorizes existing queries definitions and Info-Providers with navigation. When you click on the **New Query** or **Open Query** icons in the BEx Query Designer toolbar, a pop-up window with the following categories will open:

▶ **History**
Displays recently accessed queries/InfoProviders

▶ **InfoAreas**
Lists all available InfoProviders organized into functional folders

▶ **Roles**
Lists all accessible public folders/queries

▶ **Favorites**
Lists all queries in a private folder specific to the user

2.6   Restricted and Calculated Key Figures

The BEx Query Designer toolbar has a wealth of functionality from which to choose. Starting with a basic query definition, we'll explain in this section how you can take advantage of many of the key features of this tool.

To create a new query definition, as seen in Figure 2.12, do the following:

1. Click on the **New Query** icon.

2. Choose an InfoProvider from the **History** or **InfoArea** tabs.

3. The InfoProvider will load elements or objects into the InfoProvider pane of the BEx Query Designer.

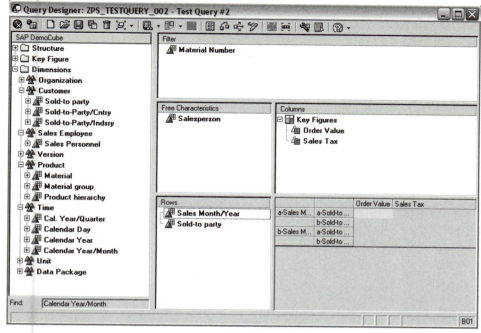

Figure 2.12 Basic Query Definition

4. Drag and drop characteristics and key figures into the new query definition. Place one or more key figures in the **Columns** pane, and one or more characteristics in each of the **Filter**, **Rows**, and **Free Characteristics** panes.

By default, objects added to a query definition are formatted based on the configuration parameters for the InfoObject and key figures when they were created in the BW system. The descriptions of these objects may not be ideal for the report developer. Other display properties such as showing totals, and changing the positioning of negative numbers and the number of decimal places, are all defined within the BEx Query Designer.

To access the **Properties** menu for characteristics, right-click on the intended object and select **Properties** from the context menu.

The **Description** field allows a query designer to replace the default name of the InfoObject. This **Description** field is displayed as the column heading when a report is executed (see Figure 2.13).

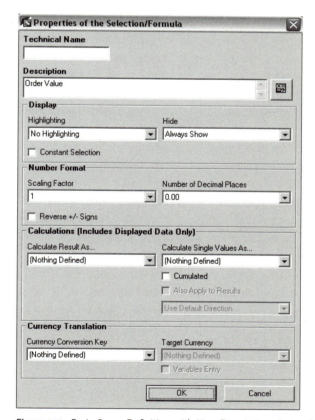

Figure 2.13 Basic Query Definition with New Descriptions Entered in the Characteristic Properties Screen

The **Display As** drop-down box allows a characteristic to be displayed as a key, as text, or a combination of both.

> **Note:** A **key** is a meaningful series of letters and numbers. A Cost Center that is represented as a key would be 12345. The **text** option displays the description associated with a key. Cost Center 12345 has a text value of "VP Finance".

The **Display of Results** drop-down box allows a query definition to summarize results based on the values of the characteristic. Results rows can be suppressed (not displayed), always displayed, or conditionally displayed if more than one record for a characteristic value is found. When creating new query definitions, we recommend that you turn off results rows to avoid confusion.

Other options available from the **Characteristic Properties** menu include access to hierarchies and hierarchy properties. There is no quick shortcut to set properties for all the characteristics found in a query definition. At best, it is an iterative process that is repeated until all characteristics have the preferred formatting assigned.

Key figures have similar options that are also accessed through a context menu. Right-click on a key figure located in a query definition and choose **Properties**.

You can replace the column heading by overwriting the text in the **Description** field. Turning on **Highlighting** will italicize the entire **Key Figure** column when the report is executed. Scaling factors allow you to reduce the number of displayed values in a report. A scaling factor of 1000 will divide all values for the key figure by 1000 and will show the scaling factor in the execute report, just below the column description. You can also format the number of decimal places by choosing an appropriate setting from the **Number of Decimal Places** drop-down box.

When defining a query definition, you may have to restrict certain characteristics to individual values, or to a range of values; for example, sales data for the month of March, or sales data for a particular set of sales employees.

Characteristics found in a query definition can be restricted to a single value, a range of values, multiple single values, and multiple ranges. To restrict a characteristic, right-click on the name of the characteristic and

select **Restrict** from the context menu. Alternatively, simply double-click on the name of the characteristic.

The **Selection for Material** dialog opens. The **Fixed Values** available for the characteristic appear on the left side of the dialog. The **Selection** area is on the right side of the window (see Figure 2.14). This is where the selections that will become restrictions for the query definition will appear. You can add restrictions in one of several ways:

▶ Double-click on the item to be restricted.

▶ Drag and drop the item to be restricted from the left to the right.

▶ Highlight the item and click on the **ADD** arrow.

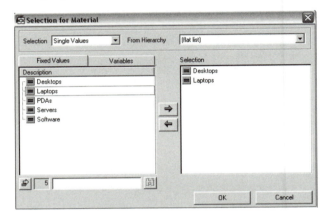

Figure 2.14 Restricting Characteristic Values

To transfer more than one value, hold down the **Ctrl** key and use one of the aforementioned methods to move items from the left to the right. To select a large range of continuous values, change the **Selection** drop-down box from **Single Values** to **Value Range**. To define a value range, double-click on the first value and then double-click on the last value.

Occasionally, most of the values for a characteristic are required. When this occurs, it may be easier to simply **exclude** the values that are not required. Excluding values is accomplished in two steps.

1. Transfer the value to be excluded to the right side of the **Selection** dialog.

2. Right-click on the selected value and choose **Exclude from Selection**.

This will change the color associated with the selection icon to red. This exclusion is clearly identified in Figure 2.15.

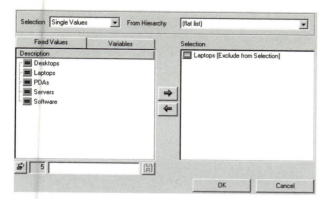

Figure 2.15 Laptops Excluded from Material List When Report Is Executed

Sometimes, seeing the keys associated with characteristic values, along with the descriptions, is very useful. To activate the technical names (keys), right-click on a blank part of the **Selection** window and choose **Technical Names**. This will add a second column that provides more information, similar to that shown in Figure 2.16.

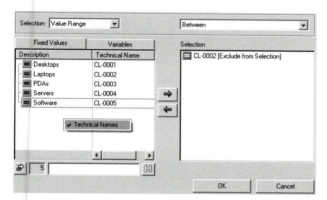

Figure 2.16 Technical Names Help Clarify the Characteristic Values to Be Included or Excluded

Key figures can also be restricted. To create *Restricted Key Figures* (RKFs), double-click on the name of a key figure in the **Columns** pane. The **Edit Selection** window opens, with the current description and definition of the key figure displayed. The InfoProvider is displayed on the left side of the **Edit Selection** window. To restrict the key figure, simply drag a characteristic from the InfoProvider to the right side of the window. Next, double-click on the characteristic and choose the relevant values. A restriction on **Division** is shown in Figure 2.17.

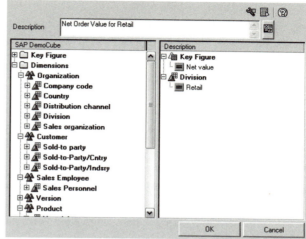

Figure 2.17 Key Figure Net Value Restricted by Retail Value of Division Characteristic

Note: RKFs are most often used to create a series of columns that show a snapshot of data with particular characteristic values.

Creating additional RKFs for other company divisions would follow a similar process.

Tip: Using **Copy** and **Paste** functionality (see Figure 2.18) is an expedient way for you to replicate and modify RKF definitions. To copy a restricted key figure, right-click on the key figure's name and choose **Copy**. Right-click again and choose **Paste**. To change the restriction to a different division, double-click on the new RKF.

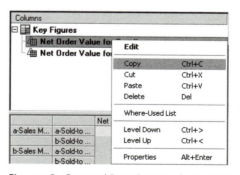

Figure 2.18 Copy and Paste Functionality to Create a Series of Restricted Key Figures

InfoProviders contain a fixed number of key figures. These key figures can be restricted by using the characteristics found within the different dimensions of an InfoCube or ODS. Calculations may also be made on these pre-existing key figures. These *Calculated Key Figures* (CKFs) consist of mathematical formulas that use basic key figures, RKFs, and other CKFs as operands.

Many advanced math functions are available. Basic calculator operations like addition and subtraction, Boolean operators such as "is less than," and Data functions such as "If...then" are just some examples. To create a new calculated key figure, right-click on the name of the structure in the Columns pane and select **New Formula** (see Figure 2.19).

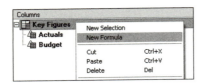

Figure 2.19 Creation of a New Calculated Key Figure

The **New Formula** window will appear. All available key figures, RKFs, and CKFs are listed in the **Operands** pane. Predefined functions are located in the **Functions** pane, and basic mathematical operators are listed vertically between the **Operands** and **Functions** panes. You must assign a name for the new CKF by entering a description. Constructing a new formula can be as simple as selecting an operand, an operator/function, and a second **operand**. Common CKFs are variance formulas that calculate the difference between an Actual value and a Budgeted value.

Once a formula has been created, you should check for syntax errors using the **Formula Syntax Check** icon in the toolbar of the **New Formula** window.

Frequently, a CKF will have a formula that is syntactically correct, but not logically correct. For example, a report developer could have created a new CKF called "Revenue Variance" with the formula:

```
Revenue Variance = Budget—Actuals
```

This formula would pass the syntax check. However, you'll notice that a negative variance would result when **Actuals** exceed the **Budget**. Therefore, this is logically incorrect, and the danger here is that this formula could

be shared with many users if this report is published to a role. Therefore, it is critical that you check all CKFs and RKFs carefully to ensure that their descriptions align with the underlying formula both logically and syntactically.

2.7 Advanced Calculations

Defining more advanced formulas for CKFs extends the value of the data found within an InfoProvider. These calculations enable you to make further conclusions, which would otherwise go unanswered. Some of the more frequently used mathematical functions are listed and described in Table 2.2.

Function	Syntax	Description
Percentage Share	<Key Figure A>%A <Key Figure B>	Expresses the percentage share of Key Figure A and Key Figure B
Value Without Dimension	NODIM (<Operand>)	Hides units and currencies leaving just the values
Absolute Value	ABS (<Operand>)	Removes the positive or negative sign from the values
No Error	NOERR (<Operand>)	Avoids error messages by returning a value of zero instead of an arithmetic error for undefined calculations
Counter	COUNT (<Operand>)	Displays a 1 if the statement value is not zero and can be used to count non-zero values
Boolean AND Operator	<Statement A> AND <Statement B>	Returns a 1 if Statement A and Statement B are true

Table 2.2 Frequently Used Mathematical Functions

2.8 Using Structures

Creating a series of key figures, RKFs, and CKFs for a query definition takes time. An efficient way of reusing a collection of key figures that have been formatted, restricted, and extended with calculations is to save them back to the InfoProvider. Structures can save the current configuration of objects in either the Columns pane or the Rows pane.

To save your work as a reusable structure, right-click on **Key Figures** in the Columns pane of your query definition and choose **Save As**. The pop-up window **Save Structure As...** opens and prompts you for a technical name and a description for the structure. There is no standard naming convention; however, most companies have instituted the common practice of starting the technical names of any saved objects with a **Z**. Enter a technical name and an appropriate description for the structure. After you click **OK**, the structure will be saved back to the InfoProvider and stored in the **Structure** folder. The **Description** for the structure will now appear at the top of the Columns pane.

New queries have only one structure by default, which is located in the Columns pane. If you start with a blank query and then add a key figure to the Rows pane, you'll create a structure called **Key Figures**. You can create a second structure in the Rows column, but it is generated differently, that is, you cannot create a second structure by dragging and dropping characteristics to the Rows pane. Instead, you must right-click on the label above the Rows pane called **Rows · New Structure** (see Figure 2.20).

Figure 2.20 Creating a New Structure in the Rows Pane

This structure will now appear at the top of the Rows pane. You can add objects to the Rows structure by right-clicking on **Structure · New Selection** (see Figure 2.21).

Each selection in a Rows structure allows you to define a combination of characteristics within it. For that reason, you should give each new selection an appropriate description that explains the logic defined for that row. For instance, you might combine a particular customer with a specific date range for a new selection created within a structure.

Rows structures allow combinations of characteristics to be defined for a single line in the output of a report. A sample structure is shown in Figure 2.22 on page 22.

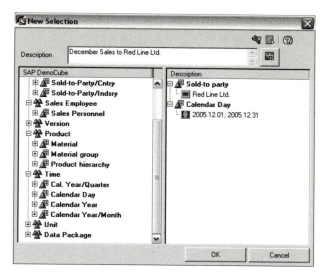

Figure 2.21 Creating a New Selection for a Rows Structure

> **Tip:** Create empty selections within a Rows structure to create additional spacing. By creating a new selection within a Rows structure that has no contents and no description, you are creating a row of white space, which helps to break up the data in a report and make it more readable. Depending on the number of rows found in a report, it might be practical to include a couple of these spacers.

2.9 Creating Fixed Query Dimensions

You can create reports in SAP BW that have a fixed number of rows and columns. This is ideal for operational reporting where the requirements are well known and the data components that make up the report never change. Creating financial statements such as an income statements or balance sheets with fixed dimensions allows for additional formatting and referencing options. Furthermore, being able to predict the exact cell reference within a BEx Analyzer report in which a particular value will appear lets report developers use Excel cell referencing, as well as construct custom reports by pulling data from more than one fixed dimension report. Fixed dimension reports are created by leveraging the capabilities of structures. Defining a fixed number of rows using a Rows structure, along with a fixed number of columns in a Columns structure, results in a predictable matrix that can also prove accommodating.

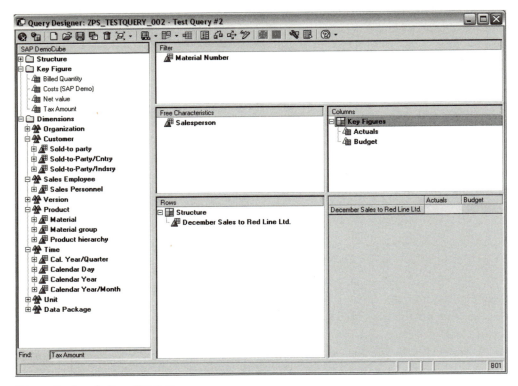

Figure 2.22 Sample Rows Structure

> **Note:** Crystal Reports is integrated with SAP BW and extends the value of BW by providing an environment that allows pixel-based formatting, which is highly suitable for form-based reports and printing. Crystal Enterprise ESE (Enhanced SAP Edition) also allows for the scheduling, caching, distributing, and printing of reports. The Crystal functionality is embedded so that it leverages SAP BW security roles and is managed from the Administrator Workbench.

2.10 Using Characteristic Variables

Creating restrictions for characteristics in a query definition limits the data that is displayed in the output of a report. An alternative to hard coding a restriction for a characteristic is to allow a variable to be used instead. Variables are empty placeholders, which get populated when a user executes a query.

Variables build much-needed flexibility into reports, and therefore can serve many more users. By employing a user-entry variable for the characteristic Fiscal Year/Period, you can enable a single report to serve many requests. Variables can be processed in different ways; however, the most common approach is to use characteristic value variables, which allow users to choose values.

Variables are created directly from the BEx Query Designer. Pre-existing variables reside within a submenu for each characteristic that is found under the dimensions of an InfoProvider (highlighted in Figure 2.23). To check the properties of an existing variable, simply double-click on it.

New variables can be constructed without programming. You can create a new user-entry variable by right-clicking on the **Characteristic Value Variables** icon displayed below a characteristic. A SAP BW Variables Wizard (see Figure 2.24) appears and prompts you for a series of parameters. When you enter a **Variable Name**, ensure that you adhere to the naming conventions for the organization. The **Description** for the variable should contain enough information so that the user running the report knows the purpose of the variable.

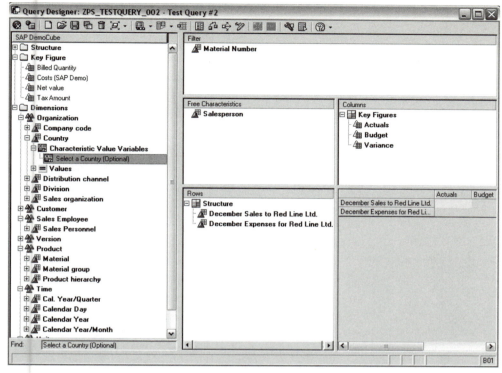

Figure 2.23 Pre-existing Variables Within Submenu for Each Characteristic

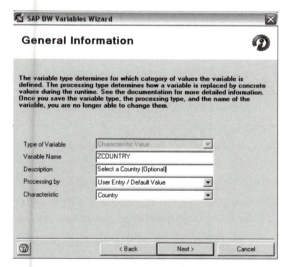

Figure 2.24 SAP BW Variables Wizard

The **Details** screen (see Figure 2.25) of the SAP BW Variables Wizard allows the variable to be represented in several different ways. A variable can serve as a placeholder for:

► A Single Value (only one value can be chosen)
► Multiple Single Values (more than one value can be selected)

► Interval (a single range of values)
► Selection Option (allows for multiple values or multiple ranges)

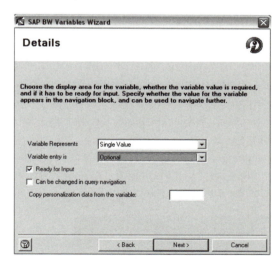

Figure 2.25 Details Screen of SAP BW Variables Wizard

You can also designate a variable as optional. When a variable entry is optional, a user does not have to make a selection when the query is executed. When a variable entry is mandatory, the query cannot be executed until a user has made a selection.

The *SAP BW Variables Wizard* has other features and options, but they aren't required to create a new characteristic variable. Click **Next** in the **Details** screen and click **Next** again in the **Default Values** screen. This leads to a summary screen, shown in Figure 2.26, where the variable gets generated and saved. Click **Finish** to exit to save the variable.

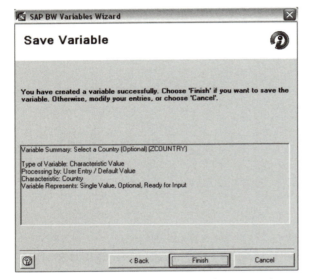

Figure 2.26 Summary of Paramaters for Characteristic Value Variable

Once a characteristic variable has been saved, it will appear in the **Characteristic Value Variables** menu. You can modify certain elements of a variable later, such as the **Description**, but some details (like the way the variable is represented, as a Single Value, for example) cannot be changed.

When a query containing variables is executed, the pop-up window, displayed in Figure 2.27, allows users to interact with the report and select values.

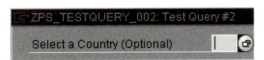

Figure 2.27 Variable Entry Screen Allows Users to Input Selections at Runtime

The number of variables for a single characteristic can grow substantially, especially when a company has many

report developers. Therefore, you should always check the pre-existing characteristic variables before you create new variables.

> **Tip:** Another feature of characteristic value variables is offsets. You can use variable offsets to increase or decrease a selected value by a fixed number of units. A variable for Fiscal Year can prompt a user to enter a year, and this year can be used to restrict an Actuals column. This same input by a user can then be used in a subsequent Actuals column for the prior year (an offset of -1).

Variable offsets are defined by double-clicking on a variable found in a query definition. On the **Selection** screen, right-click on the variable listed on the right side and choose **Specify Variable Offsets** from the context menu. The **Enter Variable Offset** screen allows users to enter positive or negative integers. An offset of **-1** will change the restriction on a variable to one logical unit less than what was entered by the user.

2.11 Creating Exceptions

Exceptions highlight certain values or thresholds indicated within the data of a report. Exceptions are defined using the **Exceptions** icon in the BEx Query Designer toolbar. The **Defining Exceptions** window is shown in Figure 2.28. Highlighting is accomplished with nine different color ranges. Exceptions are defined for particular key figures. If a key figure value falls within a predefined range, that value is highlighted with the assigned color.

Exceptions work very well with reports where a large dataset exists. Being able to eyeball the results quickly and focus in on values that are "Red" or "Yellow" is highly efficient. Exceptions can be applied to the individual values that appear in a column or to the Results rows.

Exceptions are easy to construct and are defined from a single screen. Before you can create an exception, you should know the following:

▶ A key figure or structure row to analyze
▶ A value range to focus on
▶ A color or alert level to assign
▶ A description for the exception definition

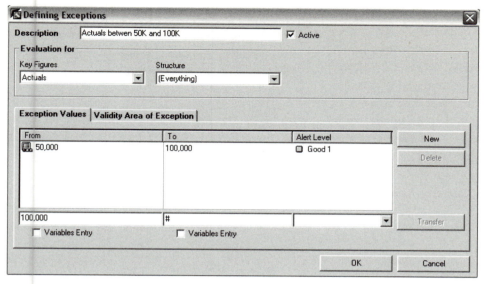

Figure 2.28 Exception Defined for Key Figure Actuals

The alert levels are assigned a color and a measure of success that mirrors traffic lights. Greens are measured as good, yellows as medium, and reds as bad. There are three shades to each measure of success, for example: Good 1, Good 2, and Good 3 are all shades of green. The rainbow of available colors is shown in Figure 2.29.

Sales Volume
1,500,000.00
1,336,330.00
917,678.00
897,392.58
660,671.00
583,679.01
374,893.08
353,121.68
336,133.03
307,362.36
244,490.23
179,759.24
110,077.97
52,669.99
17,547.76
571.00
0.00

Figure 2.29 BEx Analyzer Output of an Active Exception Against Sales Volume

When defining an exception, you should determine whether this color or alert level should be visible by default when a query is executed, or whether a report user can activate it later. The **Active** checkbox in the

Defining Exceptions window sets this behavior. Note that you can turn exceptions on and off while navigating a report output.

When many contiguous exception ranges are defined, the SAP BW system selects the broadest exception range, that is, the least optimistic forecast. Examples include:

▶ An exception range of 10-20 is assigned a Red color.
▶ An exception range of 20-30 is assigned a Yellow color.
▶ An exception range of 30-40 is assigned a Green color.
▶ A value of 20 found in the report will be colored Red.
▶ A value of 30 found in the report will be colored Yellow.

You can also define exceptions dynamically. Instead of predefining fixed ranges for each color, exception variables can prompt users to enter their own value ranges at runtime. To define exceptions so they behave in this way, use the **Variables Entry** checkboxes in the **Defining Exceptions** screen.

2.12 Creating Conditions

Conditions allow a user to analyze data quickly. Similar to exceptions, conditions highlight data that meets a certain threshold. Also like exceptions, conditions can be turned on or off while looking at the output of a report. Instead of color-coding specific values or value ranges, conditions *eliminate* any data that does not meet the specific requirements outlined. For this reason, we highly recommend that you set conditions to Inactive by default.

Conditions are defined using the **Conditions** icon in the BEx Query Designer toolbar. The **Define Condition** window is displayed in Figure 2.30. Conditions allow mathematical operators to be used that add additional logic to the filtering criteria. Some common operators used in defining conditions are:

► Greater than/Less than

► Between (a range of values)

► Top N (only shows the largest N values from a data set)

► Bottom % (only shows the bottom X% of values from a data set)

Conditions are defined for a particular key figure or a particular structure element. They can be quickly created from the **Define Condition** window.

When conditions (or exceptions) are defined for a particular query definition, the Online Analytical Processing (OLAP) context menu from the BEx Analyzer, or a SAP BW web report, will have an additional menu entry that allows them to be turned on or off. Since more than one condition can be assigned to a single query, this context menu will list the descriptions of all available conditions.

2.13 Query Properties

The **Query Properties** icon in the BEx Query Designer toolbar allows you to assign certain formatting and display options to the overall query definition.

The **Generic** tab enables you to change the title or description of a report. It also allows a report developer to change the sequence or order of user-entry variables that appear when the query is executed. For instance,

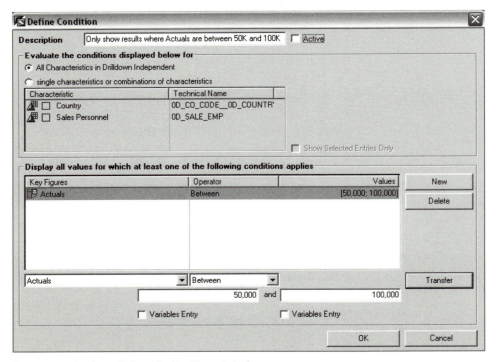

Figure 2.30 Condition Defined for Key Figure Actuals

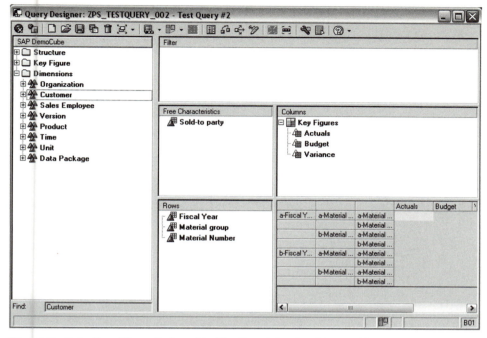

Figure 2.31 Status Bar of Query Designer Identifies Pre-existing Conditions and Exceptions

it may be helpful to have all of the mandatory variables listed first.

The **Display** tab offers additional formatting or fine-tuning of the report layout. Checkboxes are used to display scaling factors in the **Key Figure** columns, or to relocate the location of Results rows and value signs. One other useful feature of the **Display** tab is that it allows you to suppress values equal to zero in the output of a report. The **Zero Value Display** option is used often in financial reports where a debit and credit for a temporary account results in 0.

The **Extended** tab allows a query definition to be used as a Data Source. Checking the box next to **Allow External Access to this Query** will make it available to third-party tools such as Crystal Enterprise.

2.14 Summary

The BEx Query Designer makes it easy to create and design flexible query definitions that can be used by a wide vari-

ety of users. When designing queries, you should focus on performance and usability. By adding many characteristics to the **Rows** and **Free Characteristics** panes, you empower your users with much more freedom to add and remove additional detail later at their leisure. The trade-off, however, is performance.

Inserting more and more objects to a query definition will result in longer wait times for users. On the other hand, it is impractical and a maintenance headache to create completely inflexible queries that accommodate only one user.

This approach results in many query definitions that will have to be maintained and updated by a query developer. The optimal approach requires a query-to-user ratio that is greater than 1:1, but not so large a ratio that there is a significant degradation of performance for users who are looking for quick results. The system hardware, data model, data volume, performance tuning, reporting requirements, and user expectations make the solution to this debate unique to each organization.

3 Creating High Impact Workbooks

The BEx Analyzer is the primary reporting environment for SAP Business Information Warehouse (SAP BW) users. Stretching the capabilities of this tool will lead to better use and greater acceptance of your reports. This chapter will help you create your own high impact workbooks using the BEx Analyzer.

3.1 Overview of the BEx Analyzer

The *Business Explorer Analyzer* (BEx Analyzer) is SAP BW's reporting tool embedded within Microsoft Excel. When launching the Analyzer, a Business Explorer (BEx) toolbar is added to the standard MS Excel environment (see Figure 3.1). To access data, users must log on to their SAP instance and open an existing query, workbook, or query view. In the BEx Analyzer, you can analyze data by navigating, within the context menu. Online Analytical Processing (OLAP) functionality such as filtering, sorting, and using drilldowns can all be done from the SAP BW BEx Analyzer toolbar.

Figure 3.1 SAP BW BEx Analyzer Toolbar

The BEx Analyzer toolbar consists of the following icons in the order in which they appear below:
- Open
- Save
- Refresh query
- Back
- Change Query
- Goto
- OLAP functions for active cell
- Format
- Layout
- Tools
- Settings
- Help

3.2 Integration with Microsoft Excel

The BEx Analyzer allows you to access any of the native MS Excel functionality along with the SAP BW functionality. As you'll see, having two tools in a single environment can be quite powerful.

A user can execute a query definition into the BEx Analyzer tool. The data is embedded into a MS Excel worksheet. A user can filter a specific characteristic value by double-clicking on it. This takes advantage of the BW OLAP engine. Alternatively, a user can turn on Excel's AutoFilter tool and it will automatically pick up the correct column headings from your BW report.

> **Tip:** For advanced capabilities, users can embed their own customized Visual Basic for Applications (VBA) programs into a BEx workbook.

3.3 Executing a Query

Executing a query in the BEx Analyzer is as easy as opening a word-processing document or a spreadsheet. Launch the BEx Analyzer within a Windows **Start** menu and use the menu path **Start · All Programs · Business Explorer · Analyzer.**

> **Note:** The specific menu path may differ, depending on the installation version of the SAP GUI software.

After Microsoft Excel launches, a **Security Warning** dialog regarding macros appears. To ensure that the BW functionality works properly, you must enable macros (click on **Enable Macros**). The Business Explorer toolbar will appear within an Excel window. To locate and execute an existing query, click on the BEx Analyzer **Open** icon and choose **Queries**.

When you launch the BEx Analyzer, you're prompted to log on to a specific BW system. From the SAP Logon window, select the appropriate BW environment and click **OK**. Then, log on to the BW environment by entering the correct Client, User ID, Password, and Language. Click **OK** to continue.

A pop-up window opens, displaying all the available queries that a user can access. Queries are located under public folders called **Roles**, or listed within private folders called **Favorites**. Highlight a query and double-click on it to select it. Click **OK** to execute.

When the query finishes executing, the data will be embedded within a worksheet.

3.4 Creating Custom Templates

The BEx Analyzer tool provides typical functions for modifying data such as selecting, refreshing, saving, and formatting a query. The query definition determines the initial view of the query. Once executed, a query will be embedded into a worksheet with standard BW formatting. There are essentially four sections to every query that becomes embedded into the standard BEx Analyzer template. These are:

▶ Title
▶ Navigational Block
▶ Text Elements
▶ Results

The *Title* of the query is defined by the query definition properties. The *Navigational Block* lists characteristics included within a query and allows characteristics to be added to the *Results*, or filtered via a context menu. *Text Elements* provide summary information on a query such as when it was created, who created it, and when it was last changed. A sample of some common text elements is shown in Figure 3.2. Text elements also give details on any filters or variables that were applied.

One particularly useful text element is the *Status of Data,* which provides the date and time that the Info-Provider was last updated. This can be extremely helpful when you're trying to determine the relevancy of data in a particular report. For example, a query may be executed on March 30, but the Status of Data text element displays March 15. Therefore, by just reading this text element, a user learns that the underlying BW data was last updated on March 15. Business transactions from March 15 to March 30 may not be reflected in the query results.

Author	PSCOTT
Last Changed by	PSCOTT
InfoProvider	0CCA_C02
Query Technical Name	ZPC_0CCA_C02_Q001
Key Date	09/05/2003
Changed At	27/02/2003 15:45:25
Status of Data	26/07/2002 15:12:49
Current User	PSCOTT
Last Refreshed	09/05/2003 11:50:31

Figure 3.2 Text Elements Displayed Within a BEx Workbook

The Results area is simply the tabular data resulting from executing a query. Figure 3.3 shows the standard layout of a query.

The standard BW workbook template has a blue color scheme and a layout that follows the four-section format highlighted in Figure 3.4. One easy way to create more dynamic workbooks is to change the standard template. Custom templates, which are assigned to a workbook when the query is executed, can consist of additional graphics, titles, and formatting.

You can also modify color schemes, visible toolbars, and gridlines. A template is nothing more than an empty workbook with some formatting. Templates are saved as Excel workbooks and stored on the BW server. Each BW report is then assigned a workbook template, which loads before the query. Using templates allows you to establish a common look and feel to a series of reports, and furthermore, it's quite easy to do.

The following steps show you how to create custom templates within the BEx Analyzer, and how to configure the BW system to use them by default.

1. Launch the BEx Analyzer.
2. Enable macros if you receive a security warning as shown in Figure 3.5.
3. Using the new Microsoft Excel worksheet, select **File · New**. A new workbook opens.
4. Select **Insert · Picture · Clip Art**.
5. Scroll through the available artwork and double-click on an image to select it.

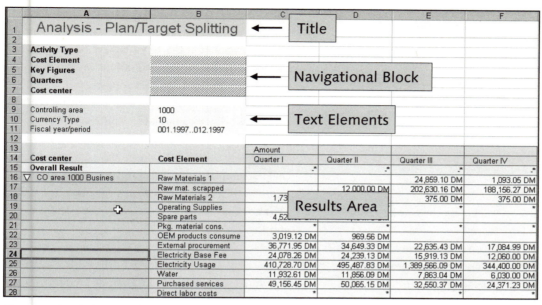

Figure 3.3 Standard Layout of a Query Executed into the BEx Analyzer

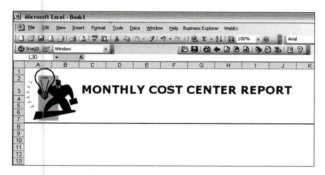

Figure 3.4 Sample Custom BEx Analyzer Template

Figure 3.5 Macros Enabled for SAP BW to Function Properly

6. Use the handles to resize the picture so that it doesn't extend below row **8**.

7. Click on cell **E2** and type the following: **My BW Reports**. Make the font bold and use a type size of 20.

8. In the MS Excel worksheet, select **Tools · Options · View**. In the **Window options section, deactivate** the **Gridlines** checkbox (see Figure 3.6).

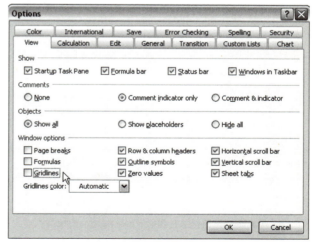

Figure 3.6 Deactivate Gridlines in Window Options Section

Your template should resemble the one shown in Figure 3.7.

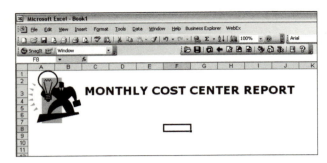

Figure 3.7   Designing a Custom Workbook Template

9. Highlight row **8** by clicking on the row header at the left edge of the worksheet.
10. Click on the **Borders** icon in the Excel Formatting toolbar, and then click on the arrow next to the icon to select a **Thick Bottom Border**.

When creating formatted workbooks position the cursor in the appropriate active cell before saving. The location of the active cell dictates the upper left corner where the BW data will start to load from.

11. Click on cell **A10** to activate it. When a BW query is executed into this workbook, the data will be displayed starting at cell **A10** and continue from there down the worksheet.
12. Using the BW BEx Analyzer toolbar, select **Save · Save as new workbook...**
13. If required, log on to the appropriate server. Provide a description for this custom template such as **MyFirstTemplate**.
14. Click **Save**.
15. The final template should resemble the one displayed in Figure 3.8.

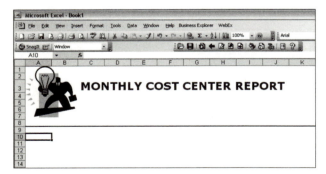

Figure 3.8   Creating a Custom Workbook Template

A custom template has now been created and saved to the BW server. To assign it against a query, you must select certain settings within the BEx Analyzer. Once selected, the custom letterhead will load before any query results are embedded. Perform the following steps:

1. From the BEx Analyzer toolbar, select **Settings · Permanent workbook template**.
2. A pop-up window displays a list of available workbooks found on the BW server. Navigate to the **MyFirstTemplate** workbook and select it. Click **OK**.
3. From the BEx Analyzer toolbar, select **Settings · New workbook on embed · is based on permanent template**.

Now the system is all set. To test how permanent templates work, you will need to execute a query. Try the following:

1. Close any open workbooks within the BEx Analyzer.
2. From the BEx Analyzer toolbar, select **Open · Queries**.
3. A pop-up window displays available queries on the BW server. Navigate to any particular query and select it. Click **OK** to execute the query.
4. A new Excel workbook appears with the customized template displayed. When the query finishes executing, the Results area will appear below the letterhead as depicted in Figure 3.9.

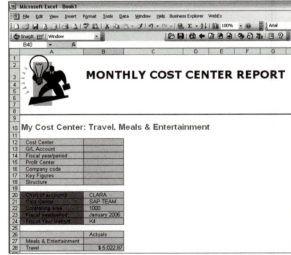

Figure 3.9   Customized Template with Results Area Starting at Cell A10

As additional templates are created, you might have to change the letterhead depending on the particular queries being executed. For example, you can create one template for Human Resources (SAP HR) and another template for Finance (SAP Financials).

The BEx Analyzer gives you the flexibility to choose one particular template at query runtime. To select a template from a pre-existing list, change a setting on the BEx Analyzer toolbar. Select **Settings · New workbook on embed · is selected from list**. You should note that executing queries with this feature prompts a user to choose a template before the query is executed.

If you want to use the default SAP BW workbook template, from the BEx Analyzer toolbar, select **Settings · New workbook on embed · is empty**. This restores the standard formatting.

3.5 Creating a Workbook with Multiple Reports

Creating custom templates and inserting a query allows you to dictate the look and feel of your reports to match current corporate standards, or to create new styles for individual business units.

Another key feature of workbooks is that they enable you to embed more than one query into a single worksheet. This feature is optimal for small queries with known dimensions

Inserting multiple queries into a single worksheet, or placing individual queries on separate worksheets, enables you to keep a series of reports within a single Excel file.

The process of inserting an additional query is always the same, whether or not the intended destination is the same worksheet or a new one. Try the following:

1. Open the BEx Analyzer and execute a query.
2. To insert an additional query, click on a worksheet and choose a cell location as the starting point for this second query. For this example, choose a new worksheet and select cell **A5**.
3. From the BEx Analyzer toolbar, select **Tools · Insert query** (see Figure 3.10).
4. A pop-up window displays available queries on the SAP BW server. Navigate to any particular query and select it. Click **OK**.

5. When the query result has finished executing, it will be embedded into this second worksheet.

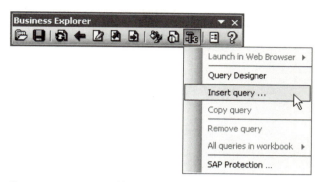

Figure 3.10 Inserting Additional Queries into a Single Workbook

You can build a series of reports very quickly by repeating the aforementioned steps and adding worksheets to a workbook. To add more worksheets, in MS Excel, choose **Insert · Worksheet**.

3.6 Auto-Refreshing Workbooks

When opening a workbook, which contains one or more queries, you can arrange it so that all the queries automatically refresh to ensure that the data displayed is always current. You can also turn off auto-refresh for each query in the workbook.

Auto-refreshing data can benefit a user community by ensuring that users always have the most up-to-date data. One downside of using this feature, however, is load time. For example, several queries within a workbook may take a long time to completely refresh.

When deciding whether to auto-refresh query results, you should consider these performance issues. If a workbook contains large datasets, it may be prudent to allow users to manually refresh only those queries that are relevant to them, thereby minimizing wait times.

To ensure that all queries in a workbook are refreshed with the most recent data, a query property must be turned on. In a workbook with one or more queries, try the following:

1. Position the active cell to be within the Results area of a query.
2. From the BEx Analyzer toolbar, select the icon **OLAP functions for active cell · Properties...**

3. On the **Interaction** tab, ensure that the **Refresh query when opening workbook** checkbox is activated (see Figure 3.11).

4. Repeat Steps 1-3 for any outstanding queries that you find in the workbook.

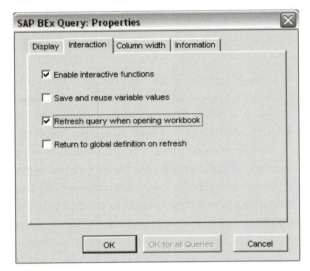

Figure 3.11 Properties of a Query Allow for Auto-Refreshing of Data

The alternative is to have users refresh queries themselves. This may be useful if, e.g., a workbook is saved with prior results and those results need to be referenced before refreshing to the most recent snapshot. To manually refresh a query found in a workbook, do the following:

1. Position the active cell to be within the Results area of a query.

2. From the BEx Analyzer toolbar, select the **Refresh** icon. The report will be regenerated.

3. Repeat these stesps for any additional queries that you find in the workbook.

> **Tip:** To manually refresh all queries found in a workbook, position the active cell outside the Results area of a query, as shown in Figure 3.12. From the BEx Analyzer toolbar, select the **Refresh** icon. You will be prompted by the message "No query is selected. Do you want to refresh all the queries in the workbook?" Choose **Yes** .

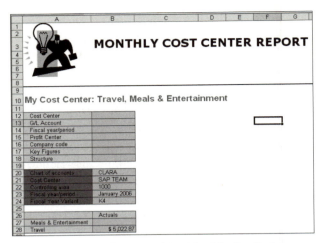

Figure 3.12 Active Cell Positioned Outside of the Results Area

Embedding numerous queries into a single workbook provides a wealth of information for users. Although consolidating all these queries may make them easier to manage and refresh, this could lead to different interpretations of the same data found within different worksheets. For instance, having two similar expense reports with different calculated key figures, and derived by different report designers, may result in some confusion.

For that reason, when designing a workbook with reports, it is highly recommended that you include a glossary or list of definitions in a separate worksheet. A definitions worksheet should comment on each query and provide accurate business definitions for characteristics and key performance indicators (KPI). Each business owner should be identified with corresponding contact information for each query. This will help to reduce confusion and clarify who is accountable for the published data.

Users can save to their **Favorites** for individual use, or to a role for shared access. Users can also save a copy to their local PCs using the Microsoft Excel menu path **File · Save**.

3.7 Using Text Elements

Text elements are housekeeping information that provide information about a query such as the author of the query, when it was last changed, and the name of the InfoProvider that the query is based on. Text elements appear between the Navigational Block and the Results area. They are grouped into the following three categories:

▶ General
▶ Filters
▶ Variables

You can insert text elements into a workbook that contains a query by using the BEx Analyzer toolbar and selecting **Layout · Display text elements...**

The *General* set of text elements provides information about the query, the current user, and the relevance of the data displayed. You should pay particular attention to one particular text element—the **Status of Data**. In more recent releases of SAP BW, it is referred to as the validity of data. Regardless of the naming convention, this text element should be displayed with each workbook that is distributed to any sized audience. It provides the date and time when data, which can be used for reporting, was last updated. In other words, it tells you exactly how recent your data is. If your SAP BW system refreshes only weekly, then your data can be up to six days old before being updated. If your SAP BW system updates on a nightly basis, this date probably appears as last night/early this morning. For MultiCubes that are constructed from many InfoCubes, the date and time shown for Status of Data reflects the individual InfoCube with the oldest date.

The *Filter* set of text elements displays any characteristics or values that were restricted in the query definition. For example, if a query definition restricted Fiscal Year to 2004, this information will appear as its own text element when the Filter text elements are displayed.

Variable text elements provide information on user-entry variables that were entered at the time the query was executed. A query definition that leverages variables will prompt a user for either mandatory or optional inputs before data is retrieved. The selections made by a particular user are carried over into the workbook and appear as variable text elements.

Selecting one group of text elements inserts them into a worksheet. If you don't want certain individual text elements, you can remove them by deleting the row using Excel functionality. You can also move text elements with

simple cut and paste options. It is recommended that the following text elements be displayed on every worksheet:

▶ Author (General)
▶ Last Changed By (General)
▶ InfoProvider (General)
▶ Query Technical Name (General)
▶ Status of Data/Validity of Data (General)
▶ All Variable text elements (depends on Query Definition)
▶ All Filter value text elements (depends on Query Definition)

These text elements provide readers of a report with enough information to interpret the data in front of them.

A query that has many filters and variables will create many text elements. By default, text elements are displayed vertically in a single column, similar to the ones shown in Figure 3.13. Consequently, the Results area is shifted down, requiring a user to scroll through the column to find the data.

Author	PSCOTT
Last Changed by	PSCOTT
InfoProvider	0CCA_C02
Query Technical Name	ZPC_0CCA_C02_Q001
Key Date	09/05/2005
Changed At	27/05/2005 15:45:25
Status of Data	12/04/2005 15:12:49
Current User	PSCOTT
Last Refreshed	28/05/2005 13:11:23

Figure 3.13 Default Orientation of Text Elements Inserted into a Worksheet

You can prevent the Results area from disappearing from view by reshuffling text elements so that they span across the unused space of a worksheet. This is depicted in Figure 3.14.

You can also apply this practice of stretching information across the unused space of a worksheet to the Navigational Block; however, the way in which you do it differs. Insert a Navigational Block between the **Title** and the **Text** elements. By default, items in a Navigational

Author	PSCOTT	Query Technical Name	ZPC_0CCA_C02_Q001	Status of Data	12/04/2005 15:12:49
Last Changed by	PSCOTT	Key Date	09/05/2005	Current User	PSCOTT
InfoProvider	0CCA C02	Changed At	27/05/2005 15:45:25	Last Refreshed	28/05/2005 13:11:23

Figure 3.14 Optimizing a Worksheet by Repositioning Text Elements

Block are displayed vertically in a single column. Consequently, a query definition with many characteristics will fill the first page of a workbook. Creating a Navigational Block with multiple columns (similar to the one shown in Figure 3.14) makes better use of the available real estate in a worksheet. To move an individual item located in the Navigational Block, highlight it, and from the BEx Analyzer toolbar, select **Layout · Move filter**. Next, highlight the destination cell for this item and click **OK**. You can repeat these steps for each item until you achieve the desired layout. Filter items found in the Navigational Block cannot be moved by simply cutting and pasting. They must be moved using the BEx Analyzer toolbar functionality.

3.8 Deleting and Detaching Results

To prevent the need for making any further modifications to a report, you can detach the workbook from the BW server.

From the BEx Analyzer toolbar, select **Tools · All queries in workbook · Detach** as seen in Figure 3.15.

Figure 3.15 Detaching Workbook Queries from the BW Server

A BEx warning, shown in Figure 3.16, prompts the user to confirm: "If you detach all queries, you will no longer be able to refresh or navigate on them. Do you want to detach all queries?" Therefore, it is recommended that you save the detached workbook with a unique name so that you can still use the original with BW. Once the workbook query is detached, only Microsoft Excel functionality will remain.

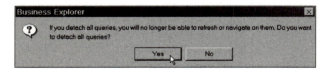

Figure 3.16 Users Prompted to Confirm Detach Request

Detaching workbook queries from BW entirely can help you to control unwanted versions of a report. Establishing a formal layout using the OLAP functionality in the BEx Analyzer is relatively easy to do. Once detached, however, the BW functionalitiy is no longer available and a particular layout is more likely to survive distribution.

If non-BW users are the intended audience of a SAP BW workbook, you should detach the workbook queries before distributing them. It also makes sense to remove the Navigational Block from the target audience, as it no longer serves any purpose. The Navigational Block is simply used to insert, remove, and filter characteristics and key figures.

Once the desired layout and results have been achieved, and the query has been detached, simply delete the entire Navigational Block to avoid confusion and raise the Results area higher up in the worksheet. The Navigational Block is best removed by highlighting the rows and deleting them using Excel functionality.

Another option that you can use to increase the integrity of information displayed in a workbook is to combine the Auto-Refresh option with the **Delete results** function (see Figure 3.17). This arrangement ensures that no outdated numbers are displayed. Take the following example:

1. Create a workbook and format the report to produce the required end result.
2. Select the Auto-Refresh option and a cell in the Results area.
3. From the BEx Analyzer toolbar, choose **Tools · All queries in workbook · Delete results**.
4. Save the workbook.

The next time a user opens this workbook, no data will appear until the query has executed and retrieved the most recent results from the BW server.

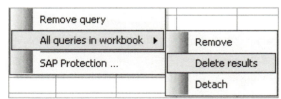

Figure 3.17 Menu Path to Delete Results

3.9 SAP Protection

SAP protection prevents unwanted or inappropriate modifications to data values in a workbook. Worksheets that contain SAP BW queries are locked from certain changes. Cell areas of the query cannot be modified or deleted, and no additional queries can be inserted when SAP protection is active.

To turn on SAP protection from the BEx Analyzer toolbar, choose **Tools · SAP Protection.** You'll be prompted to enter a password to activate worksheet protection as indicated in Figure 3.18. Enter the password twice.

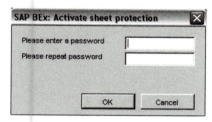

Figure 3.18 Activate Sheet Protection from BEx Analyzer Toolbar

This functionality shields a worksheet from changes, but does allow further use of some SAP BW BEx navigational functions.

SAP protection is analogous to the restrictions imposed by the Microsoft Excel **Sheet protection** function, except for one important distinction. Using the Excel protection function prevents you from using most of the BEx Analyzer functions, whereas using the SAP protection function does not hinder your ability to use navigation functions.

Note that you can turn off SAP protection in MS Excel by using the **Unprotect sheet** option and entering the correct password.

3.10 Saving and Distributing Workbooks

Workbooks can be saved to either a local PC or to the SAP document store. By using the **Save** function on the BEx Analyzer toolbar, you can:

▶ Save a new workbook
▶ Save as an existing workbook
▶ Change the title of a workbook
▶ Save as a query view as a jump target
▶ Save a global view

Saving a workbook as a jump target places the current snapshot, or navigational state of the query, in the SAP document store. Next time the query is executed into the BEx Analyzer, you can jump directly to the stored jump target to see the different view of the data results. You must first save the workbook to the SAP server, however, for the jump target functionality to work.

Global views are available for navigation or web reporting and are saved permanently to the SAP document store. A navigational state of a query can be saved globally by selecting **Save · Save view global** from the BEx Analyzer toolbar. Later, you can access these global views directly from the BEx Analyzer toolbar by selecting **Open · Saved Views** (see Figure 3.19).

Figure 3.19 Global Views Opened Directly from BEx Analyzer Toolbar

While global views can be opened directly, jump targets can be reached only by opening the initial query and choosing the **Goto** icon from the BEx Analyzer toolbar and selecting the name of the query view.

An alternative to saving workbooks to the BW server is to store them locally on a PC. From the Microsoft Excel main menu, select **File · Save As** and provide a name for the workbook. But, besides being able to open reports offline, you should note that there aren't really any advantages to storing workbooks locally.

One way to easily distribute a workbook in SAP BW, as seen in Figure 3.20, is to send it as an attachment via email using standard Microsoft Excel functionality. From the MS Excel main menu, select **File · Send To · Mail Recipient (as Attachment)**. The default mail client will open with a **New Message** window that has the subject populated and the BW workbook embedded as an attachment.

Figure 3.20 Distributing a Workbook Using Native MS Excel Functionality

3.11 Summary

The BEx Analyzer can be an excellent tool for presenting data and navigating reports. Using a Microsoft Excel environment leverages the existing knowledge of employees and facilitates their being able to access many additional features via the Excel toolbars and functions. Changing the look and feel of reports through customized templates is an easy way of enhancing a reporting package with no programming required.

The ability to lock a worksheet using SAP protection, along with detaching data results from the SAP BW server, go a long way toward securing the integrity of the information. In addition to using standard user security and roles, you can learn to limit information to only those who should see it. With the pervasiveness of email, it is virtually impossible to prevent data from spreading to unauthorized individuals; though that issue is best left for another discussion.

Printing reports in the BEx Analyzer has its limitations. A Microsoft Excel worksheet cannot exceed 65,536 rows, and there is nothing that SAP BW can do to extend it. We can argue that a report should never reach this dimension; however, it does happen on occasion.

Printing options are also limited in the BEx Analyzer. Issues regarding the width of a report come into play quite often when users attempt to print a snapshot of data. Adjusting the number of columns required in a report is one option, although it limits the usefulness of the query. Another alternative, and probably the best choice, is to train users to view data on-screen instead of on paper. While far from perfect, the BEx Analyzer is the primary reporting environment for SAP BW and it can be quite powerful when you know how to stretch its value.

4 Creating Web Applications

SAP provides BEx Web as a composite of all BEx tools that can be used to either create web-based applications, or are themselves web applications.

4.1 BEx Web Analyzer

There are two primary reporting environments for SAP Business Information Warehouse (SAP BW). These are:

▶ BEx Analyzer
▶ BEx Web Analyzer.

BEx Web Analyzer has very similar functionality to the BEx Analyzer. The primary difference is that web reports are viewed from a web browser and require no additional GUI software to use. Companies looking to save on desktop support costs may look at a purely web-based rollout strategy.

More recent versions of SAP BW have dramatically improved the look and feel of web reports. Creating a single query definition allows a SAP BW report to be displayed in either a web page or a BEx Analyzer workbook.

You can launch web reports directly from the BEx Query Designer by simply clicking on the **Display Query on the Web** icon in the BEx Query Designer toolbar. This provides a very expedient way of creating and testing reports.

When executed on the web, the output contains a Navigational Block and a Results area (see Figure 4.1). Interaction with the web page varies, depending where on the page you position the mouse. Right-clicking on the Results area brings up an interactive online analytical processing (OLAP) context menu, while drilldown and filter functionality in the Navigational Block is accessed with a left click.

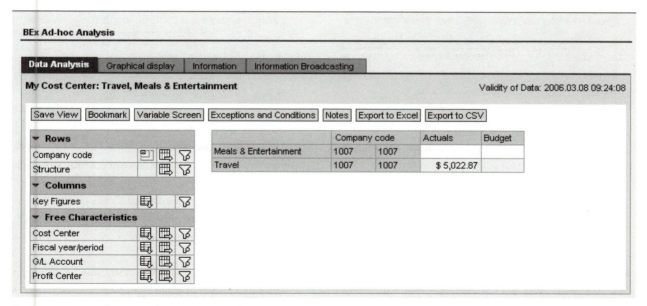

Figure 4.1 Output of Query Definition Using a Web Browser

The BEx Web Analyzer consists of the following four application tabs:

- Data Analysis
- Graphical display
- Information
- Information Broadcasting

The **Data Analysis** tab displays the results of a query in a table along with a Navigational Block that lists the **Rows**, **Columns**, and **Free Characteristics** that make up the query definition. The items in a Navigational Block are controlled by the series of icons listed in each of these sections, that is, by using these icons, you can add or remove drilldowns and filters. The application toolbar associated with the **Data Analysis** tab (see Figure 4.2), contains many useful functions like ad-hoc **Exceptions and Conditions**, and export capabilities to Microsoft Excel (**Export to Excel**), or to a comma-separated values (CSV) file (**Export to CSV**).

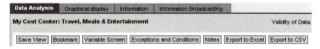

Figure 4.2   Data Analysis Tab Application Toolbar

- **Save View**
  By adjusting the default arrangement of a query, you can create variants of a report that may be worth saving. You can save them as query views and recall them later when needed. The **Save View** function prompts you to enter a **Description** and **Technical Name** (see Figure 4.3). It also allows you to save views before they are overwritten. A system message will confirm the successful save of a view.

Figure 4.3   Saving Views Before They Are Overwritten

- **Bookmark**
  Clicking the **Bookmark** function results in a new URL that contains a unique 25-character bookmark ID value. The URL is displayed in the address bar of a web browser (see Figure 4.4). You can copy and refer to it later. You can also use bookmarks to return to a preferred navigational state of a query.

- **Variable Screen**
  A query definition that contains user entry variables can use the **Variable Screen** (shown in Figure 4.5) function to enter or change the specific values that were selected at runtime.

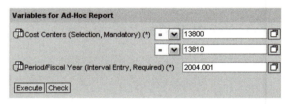

Figure 4.5   Using Variable Screen Function to Update Variable Values

- **Exceptions and Conditions**
  Ad-hoc **Exceptions and Conditions** are created online through a separate web page window (see Figure 4.6). The functionality is the same as that offered directly from within the BEx Query Designer. Key figures are evaluated based on threshold values and ranges. Exceptions are displayed using a series of colors that correspond to the Exception value. Conditions remove data from the Results area that don't satisfy the evaluation criteria. To activate and deactivate exceptions and conditions, use the toggle button next to the description for each.

- **Notes**
  Clicking on the **Notes** function opens the SAP BW document browser (see Figure 4.7). This function allows you to create new documents, which you can save against the query. You can add document icons to the Results area, Navigational Block, or Text Elements of a web query. These icons inform users of the pre-existing documentation.

Figure 4.4   Generating URLs by Incorporating Bookmark ID Values

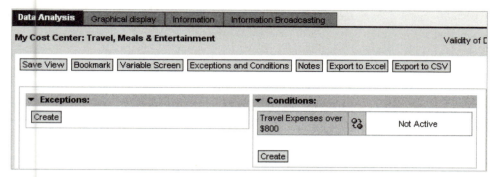

Figure 4.6 Ad-hoc Exceptions and Conditions

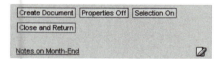

Figure 4.7 Creating and Maintaining Documents

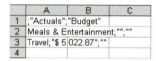

Figure 4.9 Results of Exporting a CSV File into MS Excel

▶ **Export to Excel**

The **Export to Excel** function transfers the contents of the web report into a Microsoft Excel worksheet, as shown in Figure 4.8. The navigational state of the report is maintained, as is the basic formatting of the web report. Although the SAP BW functionality disappears, you can still use Excel functionality to further format the report.

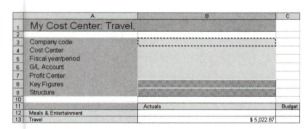

Figure 4.8 Results of Exporting a Web Report to MS Excel

▶ **Export to CSV**

The comma-separated values (CSV) file format is a tabular data format that separates fields with a comma character. It is a very standard data file format (see Figure 4.9) that is supported by almost all spreadsheet software. Because of its simple nature, CSV files contain no formatting that may have existed in a web report.

The **Graphical display** tab enables you to display tabular data in alternative formats. A dropdown box lists various types of graphs. You can format the query so it appears as one of the following:

▶ Column chart
▶ Line chart
▶ Pie chart
▶ Bar graph
▶ Stacked bar chart

You can use the **Graphical display** tab (see Figure 4.10) functions to **Swap Axes** so that the data series in graphs are flipped. You can also **Bookmark** reusable graph formats for reference, or **Export to Excel**.

Figure 4.10 Tabular Data Displayed

The **Information** tab for web reports is extremely useful. It provides a wealth of housekeeping information for a query definition such as:

▶ General
▶ Static Filters
▶ Dynamic Filters
▶ Variable Values
▶ Additional Query Documentation

The **Information on Query** section contains two very important pieces of information that you should note: **Last Changed by** and **Status of Data**. **Last Changed by** shows which user last modified the query definition. **Status of Data** shows the date and time that the InfoProvider was last updated. For SAP BW systems that are updated nightly, you would expect that the **Last Changed by** field would show yesterday's date and time. Therefore, checking this field can prove very helpful when troubleshooting data discrepancies.

Static Filters are the characteristic values that were selected in the query definition or from a user-entry variable at runtime. **Dynamic Filters** are activated by a user and reflected by a change in navigational state from the original query.

Variable Values are simply the values input by a user from a variable selection screen when the query was executed.

A single function, **Query Documentation**, is available in the **Information** tab as shown in Figure 4.11. Clicking on this button will launch a second window that returns any documents that are linked to the query.

You access the BEx Broadcaster from the **Information Broadcasting** tab (see Figure 4.12). The BEx Broadcaster can schedule, precalculate, and distribute various content to other users.

If no current settings are defined for a query, you can create them manually or by using a wizard. Part of BEx Broadcaster can also be accessed from the **Data Analysis** tab by calling up the context menu and choosing **Dis-**

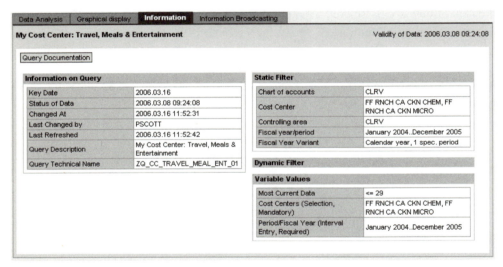

Figure 4.11   Detailed Information for a Query

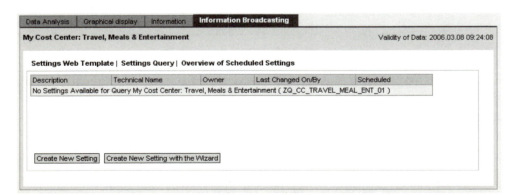

Figure 4.12   Accessing BEx Broadcaster from the Information Broadcasting Tab

tribute · By E-Mail. This will allow documents to be distributed, through the wizard shown in Figure 4.13, in an HTML format or via a ZIP file.

Figure 4.13 Using BEx Broadcaster to Distribute Reports from the Data Analysis Tab

4.2 BEx Web Analyzer Context Menu

Many features are available from the context menu. Depending on the navigational state of a web report, the context menu may appear as a **Basic Menu** or an **Enhanced Menu**. The **Enhanced Menu** is shown in Figure 4.14. By right-clicking on any part of the Results area, you can activate the context menu. You should note that entries in the context menu also vary, depending on the object that you clicked on.

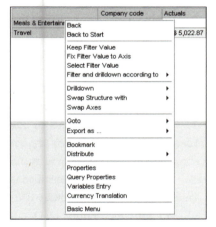

Figure 4.14 Enhanced Context Menu

At the top of the context menu are **Back** and **Back to Start** menu options. Selecting **Back** will undo the last navigational step that you performed in the query. Selecting **Back to Start** will return you to the original navigational state of a query when it was first executed. Some other useful functions available from the **Enhanced Menu** are:

▶ **Forward**

To move forward, you must repeat the navigational step that was reversed using the **Back** menu option.

▶ **Keep Filter Value**

Selecting a specific characteristic value in the Results area will filter that value and display it in the Navigational Block (see Figure 4.15). The characteristic is completely removed from the drilldown.

▶ **Drilldown**

Adds available **Free Characteristics** found in the Navigational Block to the Results area of the query.

▶ **Goto**

Accesses query documentation and any predefined jump targets. Jump targets leverage Report-to-Report Interfacing (see Chapter 5 for more information).

▶ **Query Properties**

Brings up a new window with all the global properties available for a query definition. A query can be switched to a tabular view, Results rows can be repositioned, and zero values can be suppressed.

The BEx Web Analyzer has many features. You can access a single feature or function from more than one screen, and usually from more than one menu. It really becomes a matter of user preference as to how a particular navigational change is carried out. BEx Web Analyzer is terrific for analysis and for storing preferred navigational states as query views or bookmarks to be referenced at a later time.

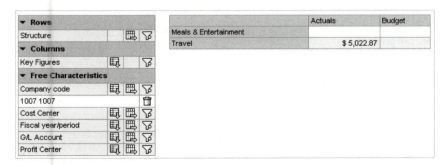

Figure 4.15 Selected Filter Value Displayed Below the Characteristic in the Navigational Block

Formatting and printing options are quite restrictive when using BEx Web Analyzer. These practical limitations are common issues for SAP BW users and are generally solved by migrating existing queries into the BEx Web Application Designer.

4.3   Overview of the Web Application Designer

The BEx Web Application Designer (WAD) is a stand-alone application, accessed from the Business Explorer menu path within a Windows **Start** menu. Typically, you open BEx WAD by navigating to **Start · All Programs · Business Explorer · Web Application Designer** (see Figure 4.16).

> **Note:** The specific menu path may differ, depending on the installation version of the SAP GUI software.

Launching the WAD prompts a user to log on to a specific SAP BW system. From the **SAP Logon** pad (shown in Figure 4.17), select the appropriate SAP BW environment. Click **OK**.

Figure 4.16   Accessing the Web Application Designer

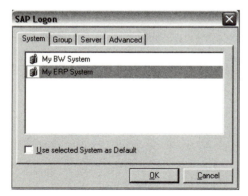

Figure 4.17   Selecting a SAP BW Environment

The SAP BW system then prompts you for valid logon credentials. A snapshot of the logon screen is shown in Figure 4.18. Enter the following information:

▶ **Client** (#)
▶ **User** (ID)
▶ **Password**
▶ **Language** (2-digit code. "EN"—English, "FR"—French)

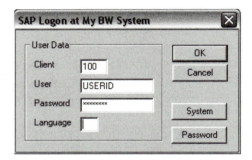

Figure 4.18   Logging On to SAP BW

Once you have entered the required information, click **OK**. The BEx WAD is displayed in a new window (see Figure 4.19 on page 45).

The WAD is a graphical standalone tool, which allows report designers to author and publish web templates. Web templates are HTML pages that incorporate SAP BW queries and query objects as tables, graphics, and maps. These web applications can be static or dynamic.

The WAD is similar to other web page publishing software, and no prior HTML knowledge is required to use it. SAP BW-specific placeholders are inserted on a page and these placeholders are dynamically replaced with the data from a query result at runtime. These web applications combine regular web page content such as text, pictures, and links with additional content from a SAP BW system.

4.4   Web Application Designer Layout

The BEx Web Application Designer (WAD) is a WYSI-WYG (what-you-see-is-what-you-get) application; however the templates can also include HTML and JavaScript. Adding HTML tags, JavaScript, MIME includes (.js, .css), URLs, and frames are all possible with some direct coding efforts.

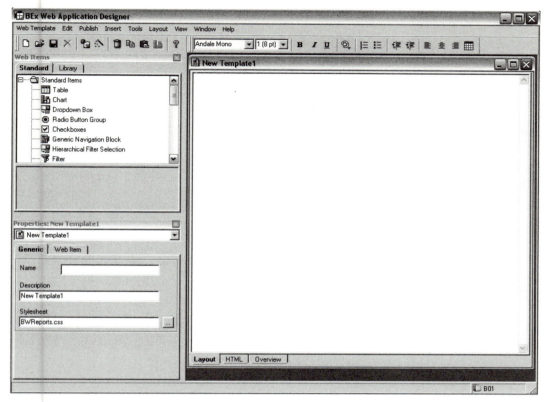

Figure 4.19 Initial View of BEx Web Application Designer

The WAD provides an HTML view that lists generated HTML code and allows direct manipulation of the code if required. When a web template is saved, it is assigned a unique web address, which is also referred to as a Uniform Resource Locator (URL). This URL can be copied and sent to users, thereby allowing them direct access to a reporting application via a web browser. Like many other SAP BW tools, the BEx WAD consists of four distinct sections:

▶ BEx WAD toolbar
▶ Web Items pane
▶ Properties pane
▶ Preview pane

The BEx WAD toolbar supports the following basic text editing features:

▶ Design wizard
▶ Chart editor
▶ Font type and size
▶ Font color
▶ Numbering and Bullet lists
▶ Alignment
▶ Tables

To insert images, select **Insert · Picture** from the BEx WAD menu bar (see Figure 4.20).

The **Web Items** pane displays many predelivered objects that you can add to a web template document by simply using the drag-and-drop functionality. This section enables you to use SAP BW data to design your web application.

Standard web items, displayed in Figure 4.21, such as tables and charts are staples of web applications. You

Figure 4.20 BEx WAD Toolbar

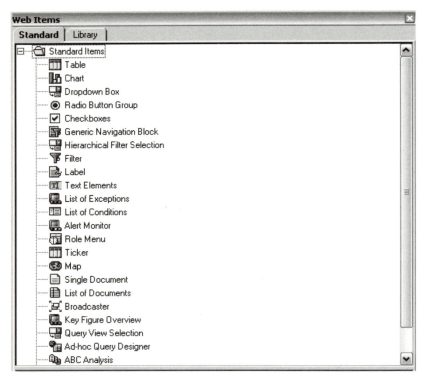

Figure 4.21   Predelivered Web Items

can make your web template more interactive by adding dropdown boxes, radio buttons, and checkboxes. Note that you must link each web item that you add to the template to a SAP BW data provider.

The increasing number of web items has greatly extended the functions of BEx Web Analyzer. Some of the most popular web items are the following:

▶ **Table**
Data results are displayed in rows and columns with OLAP functionality.

▶ **Chart**
Graphical representations of data. Many standard chart types are available, including various bar charts, line diagrams, and pie charts.

▶ **Dropdown Box**
Enables you to display and select characteristic values to filter.

▶ **Generic Navigation Block**
Displays all characteristics and key figures and allows you to make navigational changes to the Results area. You can filter characteristics and add free characteristics to the report output via drilldowns.

▶ **Role Menu**
Displays all queries available to a user in a hierarchical folder menu.

The **Properties** pane consists of two tabs: **Generic** and **Web Item**. The **Generic** tab, as displayed in Figure 4.22, is where the user enters a title or description for the web application, which is then displayed in the title bar of a web browser window. The user also can select a Cascading Style Sheet (CSS) from this tab.

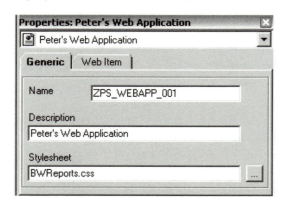

Figure 4.22   Generic Tab on the Properties Pane of the WAD

Cascading Style Sheets enable you to control the style and layout of multiple web pages all at once. Many CSS files are predelivered (examples are shown in Figure 4.23) with the WAD. To preview the colors and font styles of the different style sheets, click on the **Choose Stylesheet** button (the button with ellipses). The WAD also allows you to reference external CSS files with a URL address.

The **Web Item** tab (see Figure 4.24) is where you specify the attributes and behaviors for each object in a web template. The individual properties listed depend on the particular object selected. A dropdown box at the top of the **Properties** pane displays which object is currently being configured.

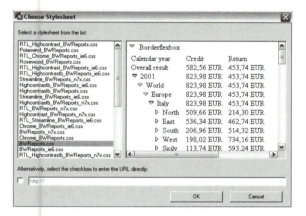

Figure 4.23 Preview and Selection of Alternative Cascading Style Sheets

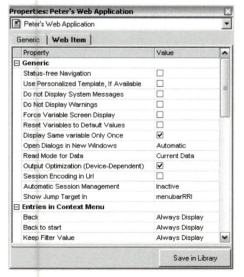

Figure 4.24 Configuring Generic Properties and Settings for Each Web Item in a Web Template

A report developer can specify what interaction or OLAP functionality is allowed by simply adjusting the entries (see Figure 4.25) for the web template context menu. This allows the developer to control the options available to end users. The entire list of available context menu options is displayed in the **Web Item** tab when the template is selected in the **Properties** header dropdown box.

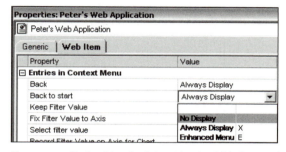

Figure 4.25 Customizing the Interaction Available for a Web Template

The **Preview** pane (shown in Figure 4.26) contains the web template currently being edited. A template can be constructed just like a word-processing document. The toolbar provides basic word-processing capabilities. You can select and place web items onto the **Preview** pane.

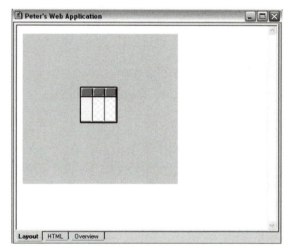

Figure 4.26 Table Web Item as a Placeholder in the Preview Pane

The **Preview** pane has three tabs listed at the bottom of the screen. These are:

- Layout
- HTML
- Overview

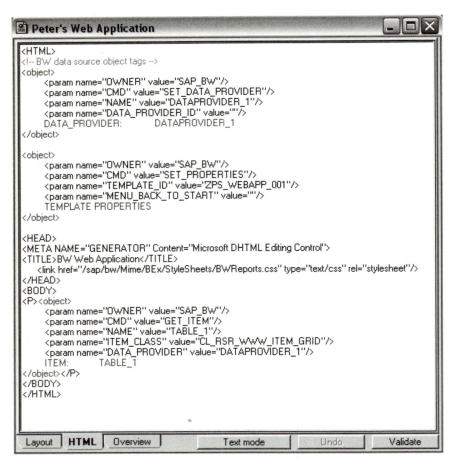

Figure 4.27   Making Code Modifications in the HTML Mode

The **Layout** tab is selected by default and shows a graphical representation or preview for the overall web template. In Layout mode, you can use the WAD formatting toolbar and add text directly to the page.

When you click on the **HTML** tab, you see the generated code that allows the web template to be displayed in a web browser. Sample code is shown in Figure 4.27. You can edit the HTML code directly when you're in this mode. It is recommended that you use color-coding to help you identify different elements of the syntax. In this example SAP BW specific tags appear in red.

The **Overview** tab, illustrated in Figure 4.28, displays a summarized list of the web items that appear in a template. Each **Web Item** is displayed along with its associated **DataProvider** and **Query** or **Query View**.

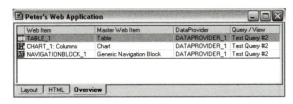

Figure 4.28   Overview Tab Summarizes All Web Items Within Body of Web Template

4.5   Creating a Web Template

The BEx Web Application Designer offers two methods for creating new web templates, manually or by using a wizard.

Manual Access

You can access the BEx Query Designer directly from the BEx WAD. Queries that are referenced as DataProviders can be viewed and updated while constructing a web template. To launch the BEx Query Designer, choose **Tools · Query Designer...** from the BEx WAD menu bar.

Wizard Access

The BEx Web Application Designer wizard walks a user through a series of steps to create and publish a web application to a Role or as an iView for integration with an SAP Enterprise Portal. This option is best suited for novice users of the WAD who require no additional functionality, such as editing code, than what is available with the standard WAD tool.

To access the BEx WAD wizard click on the **Wizard** icon in the standard BEx WAD toolbar, or choose **Tools · Wizard...** from the BEx WAD menu bar. Creating the first few web templates with the wizard will help to familiarize you with the Web Application Designer tool. The wizard follows a standard procedure that guides a developer through all the required steps.

Creating a Web Template

You can use the following process whether you're stepping through the wizard, or creating a web template manually:

1. Select a standard web item from the **Standard** tab (see Figure 4.29).

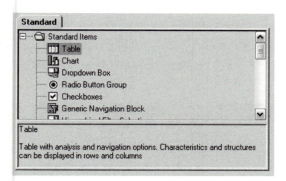

Figure 4.29 Step 1: Selecting a SAP BW Web Item

2. Select a **Query** to provide data for the new **Table** item. Figure 4.30 shows the assignment of a Query/ View.

   The name of a DataProvider can be referenced by other web items found in a template, and provide data from the same query assigned to that DataProvider.

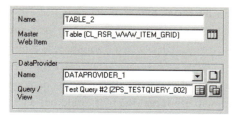

Figure 4.30 Step 2: Selecting a Query to Provide Data

3. Define the properties and attributes (displayed in Figure 4.31) for the web item. Context-specific help is displayed in the bottom of the window for each of the properties listed. For a table, it's important that you set the **Number of Data Rows Displayed at Once** property.

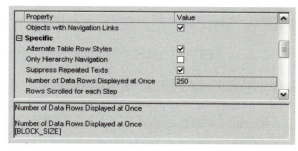

Figure 4.31 Step 3: Setting Properties for a Web Item

4. Add additional web items to the web template by repeating Steps 1 through 3.
5. Select a Cascading Style Sheet to format the look and feel of the entire web template.
6. Save the web template. Enter a description and technical name for the new web application.
7. Copy and save the specific URL that is generated. A sample URL is displayed in Figure 4.32.

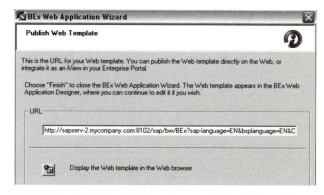

Figure 4.32 Unique Web Address Generated for Web Template

The BEx WAD generates a unique website address that can be shared with other users by pasting it into an email. The newly saved template can also be viewed directly in a web browser and bookmarked for later reference.

> **Tip:** Microsoft Internet Explorer (IE) refers to bookmarks as **Favorites**. When viewing a web template with IE, simply choose **Favorites · Add to Favorites**. This stored **Favorite** can be recalled at a later time.

After closing the BEx Web Application Wizard, the web application is loaded into the **Preview** window of the Web Application Designer. Here, you can add text, notes, and graphics if you want.

4.6   Inserting Additional DataProviders

Dragging a standard web item onto the **Preview** pane of a web template creates a placeholder for that item and assigns it to a DataProvider called `DATAPROVIDER_`. Data is brought into a web application via the following steps:

1. A query definition is created with the BEx Query Designer.
2. A web item is inserted into a web template using the Web Application Designer.
3. A web item is assigned a DataProvider name.
4. A DataProvider name is assigned to a query or query view.

Adding subsequent web items to the template will also result in the same DataProvider being assigned. This is ideal if the web application consists of different graphical representations (Table, Chart) and navigational options (Dropdown box, Generic Navigational Block). One of the real strengths of using the BEx Web Application Designer is the ability to reference data from more than one query. Combining data from numerous InfoProviders on one screen is extremely powerful. It allows different types of functional information to be presented seamlessly to the user.

To add DataProviders, click on the **New DataProvider** button next to the **DataProvider Name** located on the **Generic** tab of the **Properties** pane.

Given below is a summary of the steps that result in a new DataProvider being created (shown as `DATAPROVIDER_25` in Figure 4.33):

1. Insert a web item into the web template.
2. Ensure that you have selected the web item.
3. Select the **Generic** tab in the **Properties** pane.
4. Click on the **New DataProvider** button.
5. Enter a different name for the new DataProvider if you want.
6. Assign a Query or Query View to the new DataProvider.

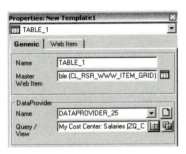

Figure 4.33 Multiple DataProviders Created Within a Single Web Application

When many web items are added to a web template, it may be helpful to structure them within a table. The WAD provides basic table functionality, including the ability to insert and delete extra rows, cells, and columns. Use the **Insert Table** icon in the WAD toolbar and enter an appropriate number of lines (rows) and columns. Basic attributes such as cell padding and cell spacing can also be defined. Figure 4.34 shows web items contained within a 2x2 table.

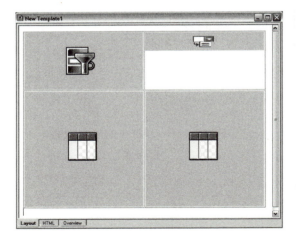

Figure 4.34 Web Items Organized into a Table

Another nice feature of the WAD is that it enables you to assign more than one DataProvider to a single navigational web item. This simplifies navigation and greatly adds to the usability of web applications. For example, picture a web template consisting of two tables, each with its own unique DataProviders and source queries:

▶ Table A contains a Cost Center report for Salaries.

▶ Table B contains a Cost Center report for Travel&Expenses.

Both queries contain the Cost Center Characteristic. A user looking at the web application may want to filter both of these reports to show data for only his or her own Cost Center. This can be accomplished by using a dropdown box that filters both tables (or both DataProviders) simultaneously.

A dropdown box can affect one or many DataProviders. This is defined by a property of the web item found in the **Properties** pane. Assuming the same Cost Center scenario, the following steps describe how to reference multiple DataProviders:

▶ Add a dropdown box to the web template.

▶ Ensure that the dropdown box is selected.

▶ Click on the Web Item tab in the **Properties** pane.

▶ Click on the **Value** box next to the **Characteristic/Structure** property.

▶ Select **COSTCENTER**.

▶ Click on the **Value** box next to the **Affected Data Providers** property, shown in Figure 4.35.

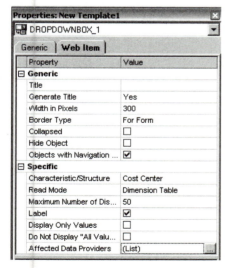

Figure 4.35 Selecting a DataProvider

▶ Click on the grey pushbutton (the button with the ellipses).

▶ Select the **DataProviders** who will be affected by this single dropdown box.

▶ Click on the **Execute** in the Browser icon in the BEx WAD toolbar to save and execute the web application.

4.7 Publishing Web Templates

Creating web templates and testing them can be time-consuming. However, fine-tuning the format of the layout can greatly enhance the presentation of your web application, which can benefit many users.

A couple of different distribution options are available to a report developer. Each template created with the BEx Web Application Designer is assigned its own unique URL. To find this URL, go to the BEx WAD toolbar and select **Publish · Copy URL to Clipboard**. You can then insert this URL into an email document and send it to target users. More formally, web applications can be published to either of the following:

▶ Roles

▶ Enterprise Portal iViews (5.0 or 6.0)

▶ BEx Broadcaster

Each of these options is listed in the **Publish** menu of the BEx WAD toolbar. Publishing to a standard SAP BW Role is straightforward. A pop-up window (see Figure 4.36) lists all the **Roles** that a report developer has access to publish and the developer has access to create subfolders for each of these roles. The destination Role/folder is highlighted and the web application is saved.

A similar process is used to publish a Portal iView. A listing of available portal roles, (shown in Figure 4.37) appears. A description for the new iView is entered and the web application is made available to any user who has access to the specific role.

Publishing to the BEx Broadcaster allows the web template to be distributed and scheduled. The BEx Broadcaster Wizard walks a user through five required steps. The parameters defined in these steps are saved as a setting for the individual web application and can be revisited at a later time.

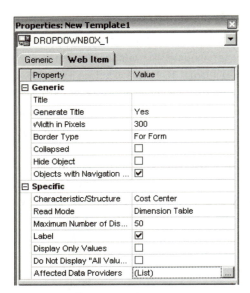

Figure 4.36   Users Assigned to Cost Center Accounting Role

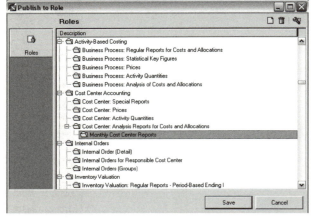

Figure 4.37   Publishing a Web Template as an iView

4.8   Printing Web Applications

Web applications are printed using the native print functionality available from the web browser being used. The BEx WAD offers some formatting capabilities by allowing the report developer to select a style sheet specifically for printing. These Cascading Style Sheets (CSS) have different font sizes defined that are more suitable for hard copies. You can find Print style sheets by navigating to the BEx WAD toolbar and selecting **Insert · Print Stylesheet.** A Print CSS can also be sourced by using a URL address.

> **Tip:** Sometimes it isn't necessary to print the entire content displayed in a web application. Navigational Blocks and dropdown boxes aren't that useful once the report is in its preferred format. Inserting snippets of HTML code directly into the web template or CSS file will force a printer to ignore certain aspects of the web page and print only the desired content, which is typically the data.

4.9   Summary

The WAD is an excellent tool that allows data from multiple sources to be combined onto a single page. The ability to make these linkages with not only tabular displays, but also graphical representations, results in a richer user experience. Drag-and-drop functionality allows novice users to quickly build and deploy web applications, while the HTML view lets expert developers extend the capabilities of their web applications.

5 Report-Report Interfacing (RRI)

5.1 Overview

The Report-to-Report Interface (RRI) is a tool that enables users to link reports. RRI enables users to jump from one report, which contains certain information, to a second report that has additional information. Some of these options are presented graphically in Figure 5.1.

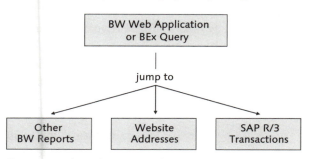

Figure 5.1 Linking Objects Using the RRI

This RRI functionality can be used to predefine a preferred analysis path that takes a user from a summary level report all the way down to a detailed document level; for instance, enabling users to be better able to drill down to identify causes of variances. This also helps prevent performance problems that can result when particularly large reports with massive volumes of data are executed. Breaking the business analysis down into smaller, modular chunks allows users to focus on variances and identify discrepancies, and thereby optimizes performance so you can be in a better position to generate high quality reports.

RRI requires a minimum of two query definitions to jump from one report to another. The starting report is called the **Sender** and the destination report is called the **Receiver.**

These jump targets are defined for the Sender and are made available in the context menu of a report. The **Goto** icon in the SAP Business Explorer (BEx) Analyzer toolbar

also provides access to these RRI assignments. Figure 5.2 shows the **Goto** menu option in the context menu.

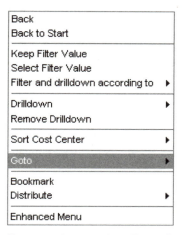

Figure 5.2 Accessing Jump Targets from the Goto Menu Option

5.2 Defining Jump Targets

You define a jump target by logging onto the SAP Business Information Warehouse (SAP BW) system and executing the transaction code **RSBBS**. You also use the SAP menu path **Business Explorer · Query · Jump Target** to define a jump target. The initial transaction screen is displayed in Figure 5.3.

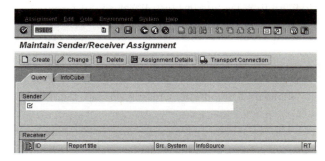

Figure 5.3 Maintain Sender/Receiver Assignment Screen

A **Sender Query** can jump to a number of different report types, and not just other SAP BW queries. Object types that can be assigned as Receivers include:

▶ SAP BW BEx queries

▶ SAP BW web applications

▶ SAP BW Crystal Reports

▶ InfoSet queries

▶ Transaction codes

▶ ABAP reports

▶ Web addresses

Usually, receiver assignments are made against BEx queries. Therefore, you might consider linking to websites that further explain the data displayed in a query and providing contact information for the business owner of a report.

The first step in creating a jump target is to choose the source query definition (the sender). Select the **Query** tab in the **Maintain Sender/Receiver Assignment** screen. Enter the technical name of the query, or use the dropdown box, within the **Sender** field, to search by History, InfoAreas, Roles, or Favorites. The search functionality also accepts partial text strings.

Figure 5.4 shows the query that has been assigned as the sender. Notice in Figure 5.4 that the syntax for the sender is displayed as infoProvider/technical query name.

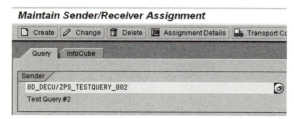

Figure 5.4 Selecting a Sender Query

You can maintain multiple sender/receiver assignments for a single query definition. This allows one report to serve as a jumping point to many other reports. To create a receiver, click on the **Create** button in the transaction toolbar. A pop-up window will prompt you to select a receiver in the **Report Type** section. Select the corresponding radio button. The receiver report type (**Web Address** in this example) can point to the local SAP BW system or to another SAP system (i.e., an ERP instance).

Select **Local**, or choose a specific **Source system** using the dropdown box (displayed in Figure 5.5) in the **Target system** section.

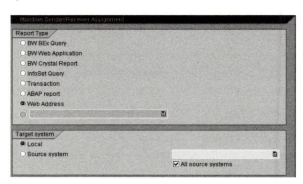

Figure 5.5 Selecting a Report Type and a Target System for the Receiver

Next, you must provide specific destination parameters for the receiver. The information to be populated will depend on the report type and target system that you selected earlier. Click the dropdown box in the **Report Type** section of the **Maintain Sender/Receiver Assignment** screen.

For a **BW BEx Query** report type, the resulting pop-up window (see Figure 5.6) will list all available query definitions. Highlight the appropriate query definition and click **Open**.

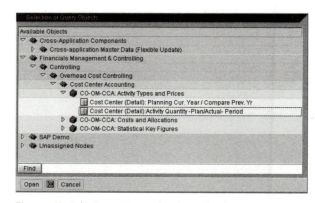

Figure 5.6 Selecting a Query Object as a Receiver

A **BW Web Application** is selected in the same fashion. A pop-up window displays all the available web templates and you select the template you want.

If **Transaction** was selected as the receiver report type, the report developer could enter the target transaction code (**RSRT**) directly into the **Report** text box. Pressing **Enter** would transfer this assignment to the **Report Type** section and **RSRT** would appear next to the selected receiver report type, **Transaction**, as seen in Figure 5.7.

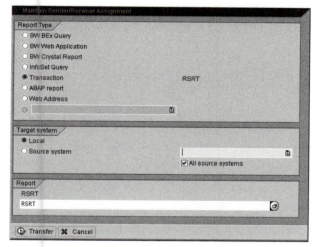

Figure 5.7 SAP Transaction Code RSRT as a Receiver

When the required information for the receiver has been entered, click on **Transfer** to return to the **Maintain Sender/Receiver Assignment** screen. All existing assignments will be listed as a table in the **Receiver** section, as depicted in Figure 5.8.

To change or delete an existing assignment, highlight it and click on the corresponding button on the Transaction toolbar. The **Receiver** tables allow a report developer to edit the **Report title** for each **Receiver object**. The **Report title** is the text, which gets displayed in the **Goto** menu for the **Sender Query**.

This report title is the only indicator for users to orient themselves to determine how to navigate through the report, i.e., where will users jump to next when they click on an element in the user interface. To change the **Report title**, simply highlight the existing text and replace it. The **Receiver object** references the specific destination. This helps the report developer keep track of existing jump targets. The completed jump target assignments are shown in a BEx Web Report in Figure 5.9.

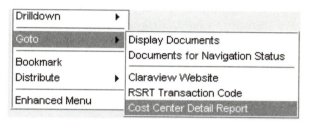

Figure 5.9 Completed Jump Target Assignments as Displayed in a BEx Web Report

For query-to-query definitions, the sender query serves as a filter by supplying values of characteristics to a receiver query. The data that gets passed depends on where the **Goto** command was executed. For example, right-clicking on a Cost Center value of 1234 in the sender query and choosing **Goto · Cost Center Detail Report** will pass this single Cost Center as a variable parameter to the Receiver report. All data reflected in the Receiver report will pertain to only the preselected Cost Center 1234.

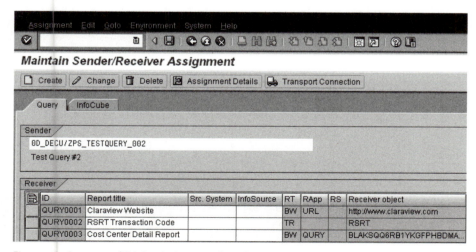

Figure 5.8 Summary of Existing Assignments for a Query

5.3   Summary

The collective capabilities provided by RRI and the presentation layer tools (BEx Analyzer, BEx Web, BEx WAD) enable users to design, develop, and publish a wide range of reports and analytical applications.

Each of these tools requires sufficient time to learn and master, and more importantly, enough familiarity and creativity to exploit. Based on the underlying functionality in each tool, it is recommended that a new user spend adequate time with each tool and learn each tool in the following order:

1. BEx Query Designer
2. BEx Analyzer
3. BEx Web Reporting
4. BEx Web Application Designer
5. Report-to-Report Interface
6. Reporting Agent
7. BEx Download Scheduler
8. Web API and VBA for Excel

By learning the tools in this order, users will understand the limitations and benefits of each application. Fortunately, with a Data Warehouse, there is little, if any, permanent damage that a beginning report developer can do. Therefore, it is also advisable that users be given access to all the tools, with the only limitation being the number of public roles/folders that they can publish to. Periodic cleanup of unused test queries in a development or production environment is a minor trade-off for enabling users to become highly proficient with building queries, workbooks, and web applications.

By thinking outside the box, and knowing how to stretch the functionality of the BEx tools, you'll discover solutions to satisfy your own unique reporting requirements.

6 NetWeaver 2004s BI Overview

With the release of *NetWeaver 2004s*, dramatic enhancements, improvements and new BEx tools are delivered with BW. The tools discussed in previous chapters remain in this new version (BEx Query Designer, BEx Analyzer and BEx WAD) giving users a sense of continuity. New functionality such as *Integrated Planning* (IP) and *Enterprise Reporting* are only available with NetWeaver 2004s. Ease of use is built upon with additional wizards, input help and drag-and-drop functionality. The major developments for BW query analysis and reporting include formatted reporting, improved information broadcasting, advanced MS Excel integration and PDF based printing. A summary of the changes to existing tools and an overview of the new BEx tools will be covered in this chapter.[1]

6.1 Changes to the BEx Query Designer

The BEx Query Designer has had significant updates including the addition of a Properties pane and message window that allow designers greater flexibility in modifying query properties in an efficient manner. The new BEx Query Designer is shown in Figure 6.1. Existing queries from NetWeaver 2004 (BW 3.5) can be edited with the Query Designer from 2004 or with the new Query Designer found in 2004s.

Some of the new features that are part of the BEx Query Designer include:

▶ Improved processing speed
▶ Object properties are displayed in the Properties pane
▶ Multiple objects can be edited at the same time
▶ A message window provides warnings and errors messages

▶ Additional tab pages allow easier access to all parts of a query
▶ Multiple default values can be assigned to a characteristic variable
▶ Objects in the Filter pane/tab can be saved as a reusable structure
▶ Support of multi-selected objects
▶ Enhanced toolbars and context menus

This new Visual Basic .NET based unicode-compliant tool is more robust, more user friendly, and more efficient. In previous versions of the BEx Query Designer, it was impossible to select and modify the properties of all the characteristics found in the query definition. This was a complaint of many users and a question that was asked quite often on BW discussion boards and user forums. It is nice to see that SAP has paid attention to the feedback of its customers.

The BEx Query Designer toolbar also has some marked improvements and additional icons. This toolbar is displayed in Figure 6.2.

The following icons can be found in the toolbar proceeding from left to right:

▶ New
▶ Open
▶ Save
▶ Save As
▶ Execute
▶ Check Query
▶ Query Properties
▶ Cut
▶ Copy
▶ Paste
▶ InfoProviders
▶ Filters
▶ Rows/Columns View

---

1 Thanks to Eric Schemer and Carsten Boennen at SAP AG for providing some screenshots for this chapter.

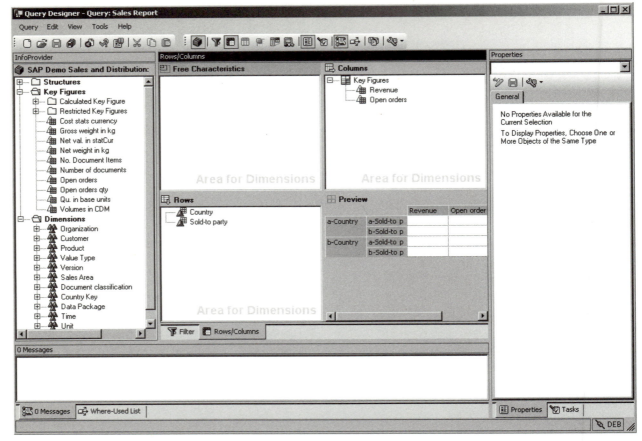

Figure 6.1 BEx Query Designer in NetWeaver 2004s

Figure 6.2 BEx Query Designer Toolbar in NetWeaver 2004s

▶ Tabular View

▶ Cell Definitions

▶ Conditions

▶ Exceptions

▶ Properties

▶ Tasks

▶ Messages

▶ Where-Used List

▶ Documents

▶ Technical Names

6.2 Changes to the Web Application Designer (WAD)

Like the BEx Query Designer, SAP delivers the previous version of the WAD together with a new 2004s version. This allows previous web applications to be maintained and updated as required without significant rework or conversion.

Templates created using 2004s are saved in a different document store than web templates created with BW 3.5 (NetWeaver '04). There is a migration tool available that helps with the conversion process but it is not perfect. If converting templates is part of a project's upgrade plans then be prepared to spend some time making manual corrections. SAP also recommends that queries and query views from NetWeaver 2004s not be used within web applications that are still being constructed with previous versions of the WAD. A screenshot of the WAD is found in Figure 6.3.

Some of the new enhancements and changes include:

▶ Additional Web API commands
▶ The Web Application Wizard no longer available
▶ XML-based document format
▶ Integration with planning functionality

Pre-delivered Web items have been expanded, removed and/or changed. The following web items are no longer available in NetWeaver 2004s:

▶ Role menu (moved to NetWeaver Portal)
▶ Alert monitor (moved to NetWeaver Portal)
▶ Broadcaster (moved to NetWeaver Portal)

▶ Ad-Hoc Query Designer (replaced with BEx Web Analyzer)
▶ What-if scenarios

Some manual intervention needs to be done when migrating web templates that contain these deleted web items. The Navigational Block web item available in versions up to BW 3.5 is replaced by the *Navigation Area web item* that offers drag-and-drop functionality to update query results.

New chart types like a *Gantt chart* are available in the new version of the WAD, and the flexibility at runtime is greatly improved as things such as the location of a legend, or the chart type itself, can be modified by end-users. Brand new web items include:

▶ Menu Bar
▶ Tab Pages
▶ Input Fields (for planning functionality)

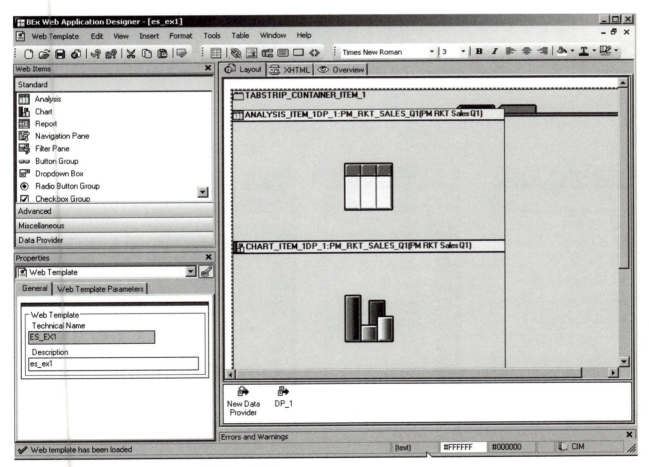

Figure 6.3 Web Application Designer in NetWeaver 2004s

▶ Report (integrates with the new BEx Report Designer)

Listings of the web items found in the 2004s version of the WAD are found in Figure 6.4. Web items are grouped into three categories: Standard, Advanced and Miscellaneous.

Also available with the new 2004s version of the WAD are additional wizards that assist with chart, map, and command creation. The new command wizard is part of the WAD and assists with using the web design API. A step-by-step procedure walks through the process and allows these custom commands to be included directly in a web template. The new WAD is much more robust than previous versions and has some terrific enhancements. Some of these are new web items, coding options, command wizard. Previous WAD users should be quite comfortable learning the new functionality and welcome the additional capabilities.

6.3   Changes to the BEx Analyzer

The BEx Analyzer was the primary reporting environment for SAP BW up until BW 3.5 (NetWeaver '04). Like the two previously discussed BEx tools, SAP ships a new version of the BEx Analyzer along with the previous version to assist customers with existing data and data transfer realities. NetWeaver 2004s allows for automatic conversion of existing queries and workbooks.

Scenarios where custom code is involved may require some manual intervention. Objects saved with the new version of the BEx Analyzer cannot be opened by prior releases. However the original version of a query or workbook is conserved for use with NetWeaver '04 if required. An example of a BEx Analyzer workbook is shown in Figure 6.5. A version of a report in the BEx Web Analyzer is shown in Figure 6.6.

Some of the new BEx Analyzer features include (as of support package 7):

▶ Integration with BI integrated planning
▶ Improved formatting with Microsoft Excel
▶ Updated context menu
▶ Drag-and-drop functionality
▶ Local formula and calculations
▶ Traceability of workbook changes
▶ Statistics collection for troubleshooting performance

In addition to new functionality, the BEx Analyzer also includes a display mode and a design mode. Launching the new version of the BEx Analyzer results in a toolbar that supports each mode. The design mode has its own toolbar that allows a BEx Analyzer user to build workbooks with functionality analogous to that of web items with the Web Application Designer.

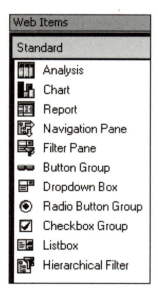

Figure 6.4   Standard Web Items, Advanced Web Items, Miscellaneous Web Items

all financial figures in mio EUR	Year to Date					
	Variance in Mio EUR			Variance in %		
	vs Last Cycle	vs Previous year	vs Budget	vs Last Cycle	vs Previous Year	vs Budget
Total Revenues	39.7	39.7	58.3	4.9 %	4.9 %	7.4 %
Total Net Sales	**37.7**	**37.7**	**57.4**	**4.7 %**	**4.7 %**	**7.3 %**
Indirect Sales	1.8	1.8	2.1	59.8 %	59.8 %	79.4 %
Sales to Other Division	0.5	0.5	-0.6	7.5 %	7.5 %	-8.0 %
Sales to Own Division	35.5	35.5	55.9	4.5 %	4.5 %	7.2 %
Total Other Revenues From Indirect Sales	**2**	**2**	**0.9**	**59.7 %**	**59.7 %**	**19.0 %**
Revenues From Indirect Sales Royalties	0.5	0.5	0.2	22.7 %	22.7 %	6.2 %
Revenues From Tele Sales	**1.4**	**1.4**	**0.5**	**100.0 %**	**100.0 %**	**58.5 %**
Other Revenues From Indirect Sales	0.1	0.1	0.2	10.9 %	10.9 %	18.2 %
Total Costs	-46.3	-46.3	-30.5	-11.4 %	-11.4 %	-7.3 %
% of Sales						
Total Costs for Production	-47.1	-47.1	-30.5	-12.1 %	-12.1 %	-7.5 %
Costs Own Division	-2.8	-2.8	-2.4	-44.7 %	-44.7 %	-36.6 %
Manufacturing Costs	0.8	0.8	2.5	19.5 %	19.5 %	44.4 %
Variances & Write-offs	2.3	2.3	-4.5	11.7 %	11.7 %	-35.3 %
Total Other Related Costs	**0.8**	**0.8**		**5.3 %**	**5.3 %**	**-0.2 %**
Amortization Related to Marketable Products			0.2	-1.1 %	-1.1 %	8.0 %
Royalties On Licensed Products	0.8	0.8	-0.2	6.3 %	6.3 %	-1.6 %
Other Product Related Costs						
Gross Profit	-6.6	-6.6	27.8	-1.6 %	-1.6 %	7.6 %

Figure 6.5 BEx Analyzer Workbook

Sales Analysis Last Data Update: 23.06.2005 08:00:21

New Analysis | Open | Save As... | **Display as** Table | Information | Send | Print Version | Export to Excel | Comments | Filter Settings

- Columns
  - Key Figures
    - Orders Sold
    - Net Value
    - Open Orders
- Rows
  - Country
  - Distribution channel
- Free characteristics
  - Company code
  - Division
  - Goods Recipient
  - Product
  - Sales Group
  - Sales organization
  - Sold-to party

		Orders Sold	Net Value	Open Orders
Country	Distribution channel		EUR	
Australia	Direct Sales	380	42.917.503	939
	Final Customer Sales	358	53.918.859	1.056
	Internet Sales	376	67.618.823	1.276
	Service	381	61.702.585	1.310
Canada	Final Customer Sales	2.724	409.601.620	5.316
	Internet Sales	2.556	878.369.244	5.912
	Service	96	12.873.600	144
France	Final Customer Sales	14.768	1.045.785.216	25.850
	Internet Sales	13.174	1.099.660.238	19.986
Germany	Direct Sales	6.480	833.303.069	14.400
	Final Customer Sales	8.400	789.022.596	15.840
	Internet Sales	16.020	1.842.635.238	37.920
	Service	2.610	70.048.336	1.080
Great Britain	Direct Sales	1.624	94.460.652	4.248
	Final Customer Sales	20.340	1.758.748.375	42.846
	Internet Sales	630	18.621.577	1.450
	Service	1.476	50.420.674	1.256

Figure 6.6 Output of a Query in the Web Analyzer

Conditions, exceptions, radio buttons and drop down boxes are just a few of the pre-built navigation components available from the design toolbar. This new mode dramatically improves usability of workbooks and minimizes development time. The BEx Analyzer toolbar and design toolbar are shown in Figure 6.7 on page 62.

The additional features made available with 2004s bring the look and feel and usability of the BEx Analyzer closer to that of the Web Application Designer. Printing is still somewhat restricted within the BEx Analyzer as the options are limited to native Excel functionality.

One recommendation is to launch the workbook onto a web page and use BW's PDF capabilities to accommodate the necessary printing requirements. The BEx Web Analyzer interface is greatly improved upon. More intuitive navigation, drag-and-drop capability, filtering, printing and distribution capabilities are a few of the highlights. Guided procedures and wizards assist users in applying exceptions and conditions on their data sets. The BEx Web Analyzer replaces the Ad-Hoc Query Designer.

Figure 6.7 BEx Analyzer Toolbar and BEx Analyzer Toolbar for Design Mode

6.4 BEx Report Designer

One of the most anticipated tools delivered with NetWeaver 2004s is the BEx Report Designer. Formatting reports within BW has been an ongoing concern for customers. Designing a formatted, print-optimized report directly with a BEx tool should start to fill a gap in the presentation layer of BW that has been solved with third-party tools such as Crystal Reports. The BEx Report Designer tool is depicted in Figure 6.8.

Features available from the BEx Report Designer include:

▶ Multi-line column headers
▶ Combining data with text, images and charts
▶ Headers and footers
▶ Hierarchy support
▶ Merging cells
▶ Standard formatting (font, font style, background color)
▶ Specification of row and column height/width

Reports created can be displayed via a web browser or converted into PDF documents and distributed. Another feature of the Report Designer is the ability to use a sub-report concept whereby a single formatted report can have multiple sections, each based on a different data provider. The BEx Report Designer is a stand-alone, drag-and-drop tool that is launched from the appropriate path in the Windows start menu. The tool itself is split into five panes:

▶ **Design Pane**
  You can layout a report with a header, body and footer.
▶ **Field Catalog**
  Keep track of what elements of a query(ies) are being used in the report, what text elements from the data provider are being used, and what free text was entered by the report developer.
▶ **Report Structure**
  Provides a hierarchical representation of the report structure.
▶ **Format Catalog**
  Keeps track of the various styles used within the report. Existing styles can be applied to individual cells or entire rows using drag-and-drop functionality.
▶ **Properties**
  Allows for the positioning of individual cells or rows.

Tabs within the tool allow easy access to each of these sections. Rulers are also provided (see Figure 6.8) that assist with report layout and sizing. A sample report is shown in Figure 6.9. A print version of a report is available directly from the BEx Report Designer itself (via the **Report** menupath), or from the executed version of the report.

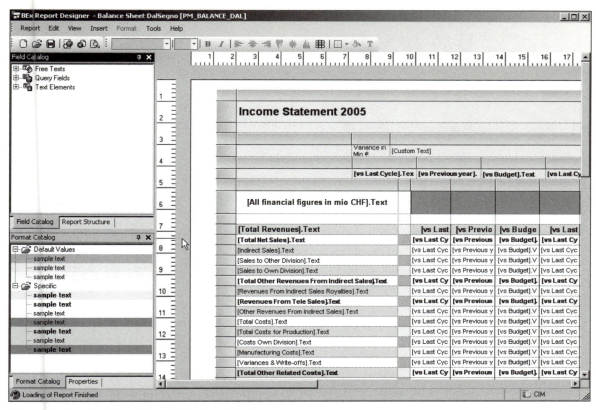

Figure 6.8 Formatted Reporting with BEx Report Designer

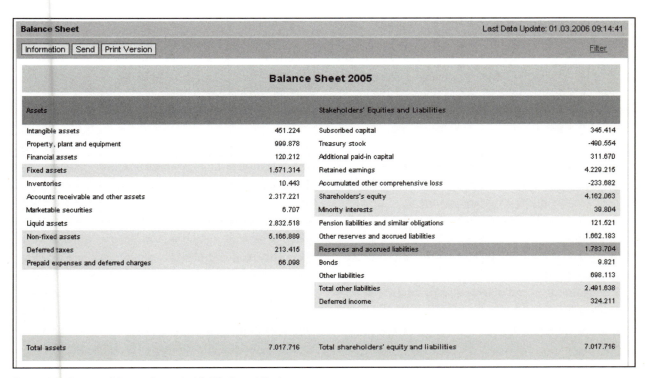

Figure 6.9 Formatted Report Created with BEx Report Designer

In both cases the formatted report is converted and displayed as a PDF document. The BEx Report Designer uses a standard web template that contains three buttons:

▶ **Information**
Displays text elements related to the data provider.

▶ **Send**
Distribute reports by launching the BEx Broadcaster tool.

▶ **Print Version**
Output to a PDF document.

The Report Designer is going to be a valuable tool as it matures with subsequent support stacks and releases. While not perfect, or bug-free, it is a great start that has generated a lot of discussion and feedback via SAP's developer network. For certain formatting requirements it probably is sufficient. Third party tools such as Crystal Reports may still be a necessary alternative, but as SAP continues to develop BW BEx tools, the business case for investing in a formatting tool will become less and less compelling.

6.5 Changes to the BEx Broadcaster

Information Broadcasting has been updated with NetWeaver 2004s. NetWeaver 2004s ships a copy of the new BEx Broadcaster along with the previous SAP NetWeaver '04 version. Queries created in NetWeaver '04 can be broadcasted using 2004s however the broadcast settings must be recreated with the 2004s format. Some of the key enhancements delivered with the new version include:

▶ Distribution of exception reports via email or by using the Alert Framework

▶ Ability to use query views and reports

▶ Distributing to multiple formats using a single broadcast setting

▶ Improved performance by caching the results of pre-calculated queries

▶ Storing precalculated objects directly into Knowledge Management (KM)

▶ Information Broadcasting replaces the Reporting Agent

6.6 The BI Accelerator (BIA)

I must admit that I haven't been this excited about technology since a certain ketchup company turned their bottle upside down.

Performance has always been a top concern. Often times a BW implementation is completed with little discussion up front on the expectations of users. Previous versions of BW allowed for fine-tuning of queries and many consultants would simply recommend staying away from complex queries and/or limiting the maximum size of a results set.

While perhaps logical, the majority of the options to improve performance are not practical, or require significant additional maintenance (i.e., aggregates). Bring in BIA. The BI Accelerator (BIA) is an appliance that sits alongside your BW database and can improve performance up to 100x without any change the end-user experience.

BIA achieves these staggering increases by having substantial memory and parallelism. At one time it was referred to as High Performance Analytics (HPA). The BIA appliance eliminates previous decisions by IT to limit flexibility and functionality of BW queries in the name of performance. Some of the benefits of the BIA include:

▶ Lower TCO

▶ Siginificantly less aggregate maintenance

▶ Performance improvement factor between 10x and 100x

▶ Predictable response times

▶ Improved user experience

SAP has partnered with IBM and HP to provide hardware with a complete BI Accelerator pre-installed. The heart of the appliance contains blade servers with 64-bit Intel Xeon CPUs and will come in a couple of different sizes that consider the number of concurrent user sessions, width of fact tables and overall volume of data. While somewhat plug-and-play, BIA still requires some administration through the BI Accelerator Monitor.

Business user expectations, exploding data volumes, reasonable hardware costs, and reduce TCO from ongoing maintenance are all valid criteria that make the BIA worth a look by administrators of any BW landscape.

6.7 Remodeling InfoCubes

While not directly related to reporting, new functionality in NetWeaver 2004s allows BW developers to change the structure of InfoCubes that already contain data, without the necessity to reload everything. This additional flexibility will have an immediate impact on existing BW landscapes where ever changing user reporting requirements can now be accommodated with much less planning and much less time required to do reloads. This functionality is limited to InfoCubes but it can be expected that additional support for remodeling operational data stores (ODS) and InfoObjects will be available in future releases. As well, the Administrator Workbench (AWB) has been rebranded as the *Data Warehousing Workbench* (DWB) and a standardized interface allows for simpler object maintenance.

6.8 Visual Composer

The *Visual Composer* (VC) is one of the really great tools available with NetWeaver 2004s. The VC allows business users to create their own analytical content and publish it directly to SAP's NetWeaver Portal. Using a graphical modeling GUI, applications can be created that incorporate BI InfoProviders from SAP or from external data sources via java connectors. The VC allows OLTP information to be inserted into a dashboard, however there is no drill-down capability as it doesn't have a link into the OLAP engine. For interactive analytics it is better to use the BEx Web Application Designer. An image of the Visual Composer tool is found in Figure 6.10.

Some of the benefits of the VC include:

▶ Zero footprint access (no software installation required)

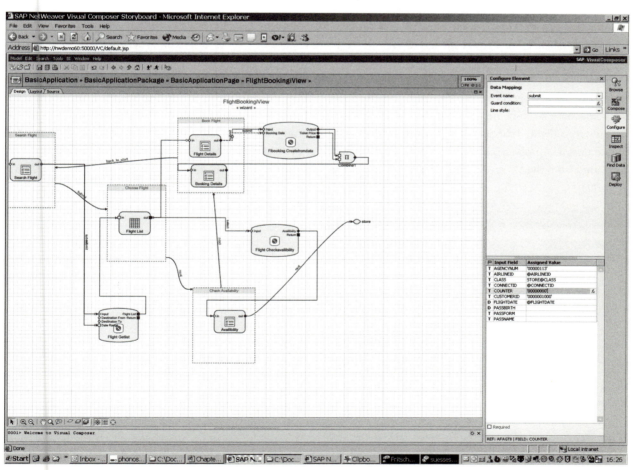

Figure 6.10 SAP NetWeaver Visual Composer

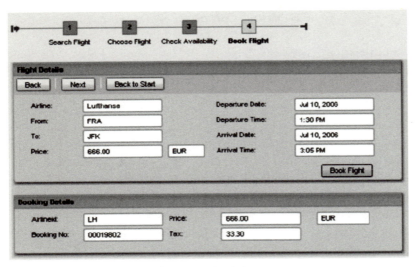

Figure 6.11   Visual Composer Application on the Web

► Visual modeling without the need for programming
► Integrated view of OLTP and BW data together
► Integrate SAP and non-SAP data quickly and easily
► Reduces reliance on IT to create and deliver content

The real value of the VC tool comes from the ability to create business applications 'on-demand'. While requiring some time to become comfortable with, the Visual Composer is highly intuitive and valuable when solving typical business problems in a hurry. Sample applications generated from the VC are shown in Figure 6.11 and Figure 6.12.

6.9   Looking Ahead

SAP has made a very strong statement with its latest release of SAP BI and its improvements to the Business Explorer (BEx) tools. Each BEx tool has had significant enhancements in functionality, design and navigation. User interfaces are cleaner, and easier to use. Easy access to OLTP data and non-SAP systems allows for seamless integration and collaboration. Existing customers will have many positive things to consider when constructing a business case for upgrading to SAP NetWeaver 2004s.

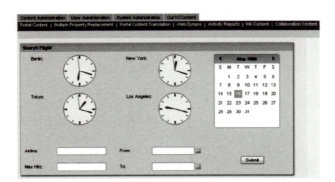

Figure 6.12   Portal Content Created with the Visual Composer.

Glossary

Administrator Workbench
Tool for controlling, monitoring and maintaining processes involved in data processing within SAP BW.

Aggregate
Stores the dataset of an InfoCube redundantly and persistently in a summarized form on the database, thereby resulting in improved performance.

BEx Broadcaster
Tool for precalculating and distributing web templates, queries and workbooks.

BEx Query Designer
Tool for defining queries that are based on a selection of characteristics and key figures.

BEx Web Application Designer
Desktop application for creating websites with SAP BW content. Requires no programming knowledge but allows direct access to HTML if required.

Business Explorer (BEx)
Analytical and reporting tools in SAP BW.

Business Explorer Analyzer
Analytical and reporting tool in the Business Explorer, embedded in Microsoft Excel.

Business Explorer Browser
Tool for categorizing and managing SAP BW workbooks, queries and external documents.

Cascading Style Sheets (CSS)
A stylesheet language that describes the presentation of a document written in a markup language.

Crystal Report
Report definition created using the Crystal Reports Designer and saved in SAP BW.

Data Warehouse
A collection of data created by integrating datasets from one or more source systems.

Dimension
A grouping of characteristics that logically belong together.

Extraction, Transformation, Loading (ETL)
Process of migrating data from an ERP system to a data warehouse.

Information Broadcasting
One of the four application tabs of the BEx Web Analyzer which can be used to precalculate and distribute various objects with business intelligence.

Navigational Block
Item that retrieves data from a query view and displays it in the form of a table. All characteristics and key figures of the query view are listed in the table, and their filter values are displayed. You can interact with the navigational block to update the results or to add/remove additional filters.

InfoArea
Data targets logically grouped together in a hierarchy.

InfoCube
A quantity of relational tables linked according to a star schema that consists of a fact table with several dimension tables.

InfoObject
Business evaluation objects (e.g., customers or sales) which can be sub-divided into characteristics, key figures, units and time or technical characteristics.

InfoProvider
Objects for which queries in SAP BW can be created or executed against. Includes ODS objects, InfoCubes, and MultiCubes/MultiProviders.

Metadata
Data about data. Metadata describes the origin, history, and other attributes of data.

MultiCube
Brings data from several BasicCubes and RemoteCubest together. MultiCubes themselves contain no data which comes exclusively from the underlying BasicCubes.

MultiProvider
Type of InfoProvider that combines data from several InfoProviders, making it available for reporting. The actual MultiProvider contains no data.

Operational Data Store (ODS) Object
Object that stores consolidated transaction data at a document level.

Online Analytical Processing (OLAP)
Quickly provide answers to analytical queries that are dimensional in nature.

Presentation Layer
An SAP BW layer that consists of the BEx tools.

Reporting Agent
Tool for scheduling reporting functions in the background. Includes things like pre-calculating web templates, printing, and exception reporting.

Results Area
Part of a BEx Analyzer workbook that displays the results of a query.

Scheduling Package
Logical collection of several reporting agent settings assigned together for background processing.

Web Application Designer (WAD)
A desktop tool through which web applications can be created. It is similar to web authoring tools like Microsoft Frontpage and Dreamweaver.

Web Item
Object that retrieves data from a data provider and presents it as HTML in a web application.

Web Template
An HTML document that determines the structure of a web application. It contains placeholders for SAP BW items along with standard web content.

Workbook
A file containing several worksheets. BW queries are embedded into worksheets and can be interacted with using the Business Explorer Analyzer tool. Workbooks can be saved to public roles or to a private favorites folder.

Index

ISBN 1-59229-086-8

ISBN13 978-1-59229-086-4

1st edition

© 2006 by Galileo Press GmbH

SAP PRESS is an imprint of Galileo Press,

Boston (MA), USA

Bonn, Germany

Editor Jawahara Saidullah
Copy Editor/Proofreader Nancy Etscovitz
Cover Design Vera Brauner
Printed in Germany